THE
ART
OF
GETTING
LOST

365 DAYS OF ADVE~
BIG AND SMAL

BRENDAN LEONARD

FALCON®

GUILFORD, CONNECTICUT

An imprint of The Rowman & Littlefield Publishing Group, Inc.
4501 Forbes Blvd., Ste. 200
Lanham, MD 20706
www.rowman.com
Falcon and FalconGuides are registered trademarks and Make Adventure Your Story is a trademark of The Rowman & Littlefield Publishing Group, Inc.

Distributed by NATIONAL BOOK NETWORK

British Library Cataloguing in Publication Information available

Library of Congress Cataloging-in-Publication Data available

ISBN 978-1-4930-3178-8 (paperback)
ISBN 978-1-4930-3179-5 (e-book)

♾™ The paper used in this publication meets the minimum requirements of American National Standard for Information Sciences—Permanence of Paper for Printed Library Materials, ANSI/NISO Z39.48-1992.

Printed in the United States of America

CONTENTS

Matt Abbotts

Matt Abbotts

The Definition of Adventure

IF YOU WANT TO GET PHILOSOPHICAL, you'll find a dozen definitions for "adventure," including the famous sentiment that adventure begins when things start going wrong. When you think "things going wrong," you probably think of avalanches, critical climbing gear getting dropped off a cliff face into oblivion, windstorms destroying tents, boats sinking—stuff like that.

That definition of adventure is a very defensible one, and probably one that best fits what we think of when we think of classic adventure books like *Into Thin Air*, *The Worst Journey in the World*, *Endurance*, *Between a Rock and a Hard Place*, and *Touching the Void*. That definition is also not quite what we have in mind for this book—I don't want anyone to have to fall into a crevasse, see people die on Everest or in Antarctica, or have to amputate their own arm to feel like they've had a good time.

I'm thinking more about getting away from your office, your errands, your home improvement tasks; going somewhere with natural beauty; and maybe getting a little dirty, a little cold, and a little tired—but not so miserable that you forget to take a bunch of photos to look at when you get home. I think those criteria are good enough to qualify to be an adventure.

Since we're not all grizzly mountaineers (or at least not all the time we're not), my bar for adventure is more along the lines of pushing your comfort zone a little bit by doing something new or with an unknown outcome. Maybe it's traveling to a country you've never been to or where you don't speak the language, heading out on a trail into the wilderness without knowing what's out there, or signing up for your first real mountain climb. Because doing something outside your comfort zone is never a sure thing, and that's why you look forward to it with something like half excited anticipation and half nerves.

Some people like to spend their vacations lying on a beach with a good book, and that's great—to each his or her own. I've never been very good at relaxing, or at least doing things that look like relaxing in the traditional sense. I'm more after the sort of moving relaxation you do while plodding up a snow slope in crampons, falling into the rhythm of pedaling a fully loaded touring bike for the eighth day in a row, or concentrating so hard on balancing to grab the next handhold that you forget about all the e-mails in your inbox.

This book isn't a list of things you should try to do before you die (although it's much easier to do them before you die than after). It's a list of ideas of things you could do, whether you have a weekend free or a month free. And it's a bunch of ideas on how to convince yourself to do those things, no matter what your definition of adventure is. There are no beach vacations in this book, but there are a hell of a lot of amazing places where you can take a book to read in your downtime. I hope you enjoy it.

Matt Abbotts

Jeff Greenwell

"QUIT YOUR JOB" ADVENTURES

YOU DON'T ACTUALLY HAVE TO QUIT YOUR JOB FOR THESE ADVENTURES—but they do take enough of a time commitment that you might want to give your boss a heads-up a few months (or a year) in advance. On the other hand, these trips are long enough that, halfway through them, you will definitely find yourself wondering if you really do need to go back to your job when the adventure is over. A few weeks in the bottom of the Grand Canyon without access to e-mail, for example, can change your perspective. So can six weeks on the Great Divide Mountain Bike Route. If you're lucky enough, or diplomatic enough, to be able to get this much time off work and in nature, you might find yourself with a big shift on your life perspective by the end of your trip—which is kind of the whole point on doing a big thing, isn't it?

#1

Ride the Great Divide Mountain Bike Route

LENGTH: Quit Your Job

DESCRIPTION: If you've ever thought about riding your bicycle across America but weren't in love with the idea of sharing the road with hundreds of cars, the Great Divide Mountain Bike Route might be for you. Rolling along the Continental Divide, the route begins in Banff, Alberta, Canada, and finishes in Antelope Wells, New Mexico (on the US–Mexico border), covering 2,768 miles of terrain, most of it unpaved.

On the route, you'll cross the Continental Divide 30 times and climb more than 200,000 feet. It's 90 percent unpaved, mostly dirt roads with a small amount of single-track, as it runs through Alberta, British Columbia, Montana, Idaho, Wyoming, Colorado, and New Mexico. It's not only a challenge of endurance but also of route finding—it's not officially signed, and at times, you'll go more than 100 miles between water and food sources. Oh, and you might see the occasional bear—but maybe just pronghorn and antelope.

Participants in the Tour Divide race start their attempts in mid-June of each year and finish in 2 to 3 weeks—which requires pedaling more than 125 miles per day. To ride the route at a more leisurely pace (and have time to take more photos), plan on at least 6 weeks (and add a little extra time to get yourself and your bike to and from the start and end points). You'll need a reliable mountain bike or cyclocross bike, bike-packing bags or a trailer, some solid bike maintenance/repair knowledge in case of minor mechanical problems in the middle of nowhere, and the fortitude for some long days in the saddle.

SEASON: Late June–Sept

INFO: adventurecycling.org

Mike Deme

Raft the Colorado River Through the Grand Canyon, Arizona

LENGTH: Quit Your Job

DESCRIPTION: Millions of people visit the Grand Canyon each year, but most see it only from viewpoints on the South Rim—and only 10,000 people each year get to see it from the bottom of the canyon, on the seat of a nonmotorized boat. The difference? Many visitors spend only a few minutes at the South Rim, and seeing it from the bottom on a boat takes anywhere from 12 to 28 days. Oh, and most people who have been on a Grand Canyon raft trip will probably tell you it was an experience of a lifetime—luxury beach camping, 277 miles of river travel with more than 40 rapids rated 5 or higher on the Grand Canyon's own 1–10 whitewater rating scale, millions of years of geological history, and no cell phone signal (that's right).

  Most guided Grand Canyon boat trips take between 12 and 16 days and run April through October. Every day, you'll ride on a raft or a wooden dory rowed by a skilled guide, who will ideally keep the boat from flipping in all those rapids (which they usually do, but there are no guarantees), and you'll stop to hike up some of the dozens of side canyons that line the Grand. Every night, you'll have dinner and drink and sleep under the stars on a beach on the riverbank as the Colorado flows by. At the take-out, you'll very likely think it was the best camping trip you've ever had.

SEASON: Apr–Oct

INFO: oars.com/grandcanyon

© iStock.com/tonda

The Hardest Thing Is Convincing Yourself It's Okay

© iStock.com/Rex_Wholster

YOU PROBABLY FEEL LIKE YOU'RE PULLED in a million different directions: Work, family, home maintenance/improvement, yard work—the list never ends. Even if we don't have a lot of commitments, a lot of us find it difficult to take time off work (Americans are statistically very bad at it). So it's hard to look at an adventure and tell yourself you deserve a few weeks, a week, or even just a weekend off to go do something in the wilderness.

But listen when I tell you that you need something to put in your end-of-year holiday cards. If you don't send cards, you need something to look back on at the end of the year—besides all those commitments in life. It's great to do your job and keep the gutters clean and the yard trimmed, but no one gets to the end of their year and says, "Wow, what a great year—I mowed my lawn every Saturday like clockwork!" Plenty of folks do, however, look back at photos of their hikes, weekend trips to new cities, and vacations and smile.

You have to first convince yourself you are worth it and then follow through with everyone else in your life. In many circles, this is called "self-care": the idea that we need to take care of ourselves in order to lead productive lives. Usually, self-care deals with sleep, nutrition, and exercise, but plenty of people will tell you that getting out of your routine is a part of self-care as well. To me, that means having an adventure, whether it's for a day or a month. (Let's be honest: Most of us can envision taking a day off more than a month off.)

So talk yourself into it first. It may be setting aside a couple of weekends each summer for your own adventure dreams, taking a Friday off to travel somewhere new for the weekend, or taking a Tuesday off to go skiing or hiking. Yes, you might get paid for those unused vacation days at the end of the year, but there are few things that you can buy with that money that are worth getting out of the office instead. It's easy to get stuck in a rut where you're working hard for everyone else and neglecting the things you want and need—like spending the night sleeping under the stars or going for a long hike—so you have to recognize it and schedule some time out of the rut for yourself.

Now I know you're important at work and at home, but trust me, the folks at work and at home can do without you for a day or a couple days. Although it's tough to imagine, one day the world will keep going on without you in it and will do so for many years. You'd be surprised what people do when you're unavailable for a day or two: They figure it out on their own. Yes, if you were there, you could have helped (or maybe even done it better), but don't think about that. Think about self-care and schedule some time for yourself.

#3

Thru-Hike the Appalachian Trail

LENGTH: Quit Your Job

DESCRIPTION: Do you like backpacking? Then you'll love the Appalachian Trail, the longest hiking-only trail in the world, which offers prospective suitors 2,190 miles of hiking from Springer Mountain, Georgia, to the summit of Mount Katahdin in Maine. That's about 5 million bootsteps, which takes most thru-hikers 6 months to complete. To hike the entire trail, you have to quit your job, already be unemployed, or be really good at taking conference calls while huffing and puffing your way up the next hill, carrying everything you need in your backpack.

The good news is walking every day for 6 months will probably get you in the best physical shape of your life. Oh, and the scenery of one of the world's oldest mountain ranges isn't half bad, if you enjoy rushing creeks as well as mountainsides and valleys packed with deciduous and evergreen trees. And you'll have company: Around 2,500 to 3,000 hikers start the Appalachian Trail each year, but only one in four hikers finishes. Injuries are a common reason for ending a thru-hike, as is running out of money—most hikers will spend $1,000 per month on the trail.

The United States now has three long-distance trails running north to south, including the Pacific Crest Trail on the West Coast and the Continental Divide Trail through the Rocky Mountains—but the original is the Appalachian Trail, conceived in 1921 and completed in 1937 (and first thru-hiked in 1936, before it was finished).

SEASON: Apr–Oct

INFO: appalachiantrail.org

Thru-Hike the Pacific Crest Trail

LENGTH: Quit Your Job

DESCRIPTION: After Cheryl Strayed wrote her best-selling book *Wild* about her trek on the Pacific Crest Trail (not to mention the 2014 movie of the same name starring Reese Witherspoon), the PCT rose to prominence alongside its older, more established sister trail, the Appalachian Trail.

   The trails are similar in that they require tremendous amounts of time and effort—most people take 6 months to hike the PCT or the AT, carrying everything they need in a backpack. But the scenery on the PCT is far different from that of the AT: The PCT begins in the Southern California desert, then climbs into the clean granite of the Sierra Nevada (home to the highest mountain in the Lower 48, 14,505-foot Mount Whitney), then into the deep forests of the Pacific Northwest in Oregon and Washington. PCT thru-hikers often use mountaineering axes to cross snowfields in the Sierra, camp in the wild almost every night, and cross large swaths of desert between water sources. Over its 2,659 miles, the PCT takes hikers up to elevations of 13,153 feet and as low as barely above sea level.

   Some thru-hikers don't have to choose which long-distance trail they want to experience—once they have been bitten by the bug on the AT, the PCT, or the Continental Divide Trail, they tackle the others and complete America's Triple Crown. This, of course, requires three summers for most people and also seasonal employment, a liberal vacation policy, or a very understanding boss at work. But if you're going to go on a backpacking trip, why not go on a big one?

SEASON: Late Apr–Sept

INFO: pcta.org

© iStock.com/UT07

Expanding Your
"Adventure Spectrum"

© iStock.com/eppicphotography

VERY EARLY IN MY LIFE OF EXPLORING THE OUTDOORS, I worked at an outdoor shop. I was excited about hiking and backpacking and climbing nontechnical mountains. But my coworkers were set on taking me rock climbing. I wasn't having any of it. I gave them excuses: No thanks, I'm not some sort of adrenaline junkie, or I'm scared of heights, or I'm just fine hiking in beautiful places.

Finally, I relented and went climbing with them one day. It was just like I thought it would be: terrifying. I hated it. I went a handful of times and never got comfortable, and then I packed away my climbing shoes and harness for a year while I did other things in the outdoors. A year later, I tried climbing again, and something about it took this time. I liked it. Was I still scared of heights? Hell yes. Was it debilitating? Not quite.

A decade later, I had climbed all over the West and Europe, pushing myself to deal with fear in some very real situations. I became comfortable standing on cliff edges hundreds of feet off the ground. I was aware of heights but less afraid of them. I was functioning instead of shaking and hyperventilating. Instead of backing away from something I was scared of, I went to it to learn how to manage fear.

I believe adventure can be dealt with the same way. Lots of things are scary the first time: sleeping in a tent (what about bears?), going hiking (what about lightning?), or traveling to a new country (will anyone understand me?). You can live in fear of everything and never go outside, or you can go see for yourself what it's like. Most of the time, I believe people tackle things they are anxious about and afterward say to themselves, "Well, that wasn't so bad after all."

I think everyone exists on a spectrum of adventure from "Not Adventurous at All" (i.e., never doing anything out of our daily routine) to "Extremely Adventurous" (i.e., war reporter, climbing K2 in winter). I think with every new thing we try, we push ourselves a little more toward the "Extremely Adventurous" end of the spectrum, collecting "That Wasn't So Bad After All" experiences along the way—not to mention collecting some wonderful memories of new places, new people, and new things we learn about ourselves. I personally used my rock climbing experiences to deal with a fear of public speaking (something many people share): I told myself I had done many things without certain outcomes before and survived, so why should public speaking be any different? It took about a dozen experiences before I was comfortable going up in front of a group of people and telling my stories, but just like rock climbing, exposure lessened the anxiety.

You don't have to become a rock climber, war reporter, or climb K2 in the winter to experience the joy of new adventures. You just have to start with something you're a little scared of. Maybe it's traveling to the Galapagos Islands, trying mountain biking for the first time, or finally asking your boss for 3 straight weeks of vacation so you can hike the John Muir Trail. Whatever it is, trying something you're curious about (but also worried about) can be incredibly rewarding and can open you up to even more new experiences.

#5

Climb Denali, Alaska

LENGTH: Quit Your Job

DESCRIPTION: If you visit Alaska with hopes of seeing Denali, the highest summit in North America, you might hear from locals that on any given summer day, your chances of seeing the mountain are about 50-50. It's so big, it creates its own weather, so it's often hidden behind a cloud. Seeing it is hard enough, and climbing it is no walk in the park—only a few hundred people get to the summit each year.

Denali's 20,320-foot summit doesn't come easily—or quickly. You'll need about 3 weeks off work just to attempt the climb, including flying to Alaska, getting flown to the Kahiltna Glacier where the climb begins, and then several days of hiking gear higher up the mountain and waiting for good weather to attempt a summit bid. And that's not all—most guide services won't take clients on Denali if they haven't had at least some mountaineering experience. Guides will require climbers to have mountaineering skills, usually acquired through a multiday mountaineering field seminar or a guided climb of a peak like Mount Rainier.

The good news is, the climb itself isn't that technical—just snow climbing and lots of travel on snow to get to the climbing. You'll climb to the top of one of the most famous peaks in the world and have views unlike anywhere else. Denali is the third most prominent and third most isolated mountain on earth behind Mount Everest and Argentina's Mount Aconcagua, meaning it doesn't have very many high mountains as neighbors. Beautiful, yes, but not nearly as high, so once you're on top of Denali, the views don't quit.

SEASON: May–June

INFO: climbalaska.org

Bicycle the TransAmerica Trail, USA

LENGTH: Quit Your Job

DESCRIPTION: Traveling at 11 mph by bicycle is the perfect speed: slower than a car, which blows by everything at 65 mph or more, but way faster than walking. And, there's coasting downhill. You don't use any fuel other than all the food you have to put in your body (which is tasty). If you want to see the United States of America—while getting some exercise—bicycling is the way to do it.

There's no one set way to bicycle across the states, but the Adventure Cycling Association's TransAmerica Trail was the first bicycle touring route to cross the country, mapped and finished in 1976. It's 4,228 miles, and usually takes cyclists around 2.5 months to complete (if you do the math, that's an average of 56 miles a day if you ride every single day for 75 days). But there's no set time limit, of course, and many cyclists take longer to do it. You can carry all your gear with you and camp the entire way, carry minimal gear and stay in hotels every night, or even have a friend or spouse drive a support vehicle and meet you every evening.

On the TransAmerica Trail, you'll start in Astoria, Oregon, on the coast of the Pacific Ocean, and end in Yorktown, Virginia, riding mostly rural two-lane highways the entire way. You'll ride through Yellowstone and Grand Teton National Parks, pass Mammoth Cave National Park in Kentucky, and ride part of the Blue Ridge Parkway in Virginia on your way to the East Coast. Touring cyclists usually burn 4,000 to 8,000 calories per day, so be prepared to eat lots of pie along the way.

SEASON: May–Sept

INFO: adventurecycling.org

Rachel Stevens

Five Ways to Save Money
on Road Trips

© iStock.com/cookelma

1. **BRING YOUR OWN FOOD.** Yes, this sounds like an obvious idea, but many of
   us forget it. How many times have you been hungry on the road, searched for a
   restaurant, settled for something that wasn't that great, and then wished (even
   just a little bit) that you hadn't spent $25–30 on an underwhelming meal? I don't
   know about you, but I haven't been that disappointed in many of the sandwiches
   I've made for myself, and I certainly never get the feeling that I didn't get my
   money's worth.

2. **BRING A FORK, SPOON, AND BOWL WITH YOU AND KEEP THEM HANDY.** Someone once told me the first rule of being a dirtbag is "Always have a spoon," so you never miss out on free food. Having eating utensils with you means you don't have to rely on convenience foods, which are usually expensive and not that healthy for you. If you have a fork, you can pop into a grocery store and make yourself a salad in the parking lot. If you have a spoon, you can make yourself a peanut butter and jelly sandwich in the same parking lot. And so on.

3. **DON'T SHOWER EVERY DAY.** In real life, showers are necessary to not offend your coworkers, friends, and family. On the road, they're a luxury and can be pretty costly. Think about it: If you need to shower every day, you need to get a hotel almost every single night, and that's (in a very inexpensive hotel) at least $65 per day. If you find public showers somewhere (at a rec center or a campground), they're more like $5–10 but can still put a major hitch in your day. Learn to be low-maintenance and you'll be more efficient and save money. In years of road-tripping around the West, I've discovered that taking a shower every few days and doing a little triage in between showers is just fine and keeps the focus where it should be: on having fun and seeing as much as possible.

4. **LEARN TO STAY IN A TENT INSTEAD OF A HOTEL.** You can grab a tent spot at most campgrounds for $20 or less. Traveling in a car or truck and sleeping in a tent is way cheaper than the alternatives of hotels (finding a new home every night) or RVs (bringing your home with you everywhere, paying for way more gas, and paying more for hookups).

5. **DON'T PAY FOR WATER.** That's right. Buying bottled water is not only terrible for the environment, but it's also ridiculously expensive. There's enough free water out there that you should almost never have to pay for it. Just buy a few 1-gallon jugs of water ($1.35 each at any grocery store), and keep them with you to refill when you're traveling and camping. Once you start looking, you'll have no trouble finding the free water spigots at campgrounds, national parks, tourist town visitor centers, and even truck stops along the interstate. And you won't be throwing away dozens of plastic bottles throughout your trip.

Thru-Hike the John Muir Trail, California

LENGTH: Quit Your Job

DESCRIPTION: If it weren't for a Scottish immigrant named John Muir who spent all his spare time falling in love with nature and writing about it in the late 1800s and early 1900s, we might not know California's Sierra Nevada as the "Range of Light." His namesake trail in the Sierra is a backpacker's life-list trip, a 211-mile tour of the clean granite peaks and alpine lakes that he made famous in his writings.

The JMT is no beginner's trek, with 47,000 feet of cumulative elevation gain and 3 weeks of daily hiking while carrying everything you need on your back. You won't have to carry all your food and fuel for the entire 3 weeks at once—there are several resupply points along the way where you can ship your food and fuel in advance.

On a thru-hike of the JMT, you'll cross eight high mountain passes, stand on two iconic summits (Half Dome and Mount Whitney), and walk through three national parks: Sequoia, Kings Canyon, and Yosemite. Almost all of the trail is in wilderness, and about a third of it is above 10,000 feet. But the scenery is some of the most beautiful—and famous —in the Lower 48. A thru-hike of the JMT is an unforgettable experience and much more manageable than a 6-month thru-hike of the Appalachian Trail or the Pacific Crest Trail.

SEASON: July–Sept

INFO: johnmuirtrail.org

Backpack the Colorado Trail, Colorado

LENGTH: Quit Your Job

DESCRIPTION: If you haven't spent much time there, you might not know how different the mountains in Colorado's Front Range are from the San Juans in southwest Colorado—but the Colorado Trail is designed to show you just that, from the rolling ridgelines on the eastern side of the Continental Divide near Denver to the rugged pinnacles of the San Juans in the historic mining country around Silverton and Durango, almost 500 trail miles away.

The 488-mile trail crosses eight mountain ranges and five river systems on its way across the state, beginning just outside of Denver in the foothills and ending in the town of Durango. The total elevation gain for a thru-hike is about 89,000 feet, or roughly three Mount Everests stacked on top of each other. The average elevation of the trail is 10,347 feet, although there are plenty of dips below treeline to offer shelter from Colorado's infamous afternoon mountain thunderstorms. You won't be carrying all your food for 5 weeks, as the trail passes through plenty of small towns where you can pick up resupply packages you've mailed to yourself. There are also plenty of opportunities to hitchhike or take buses into towns with hotels and grocery stores.

Most hikers take 4 to 6 weeks to complete the trail during the summer months (which makes it perfect if you're an education professional with summers off), so it's not quite as huge a commitment as the Appalachian Trail or the Pacific Crest Trail, but it is long enough to be the hike of a lifetime.

SEASON: July–late Sept

INFO: coloradotrail.org

Christina Fawn

The More You Know,
the Less You Need

Ben Kraushaar

THERE'S A SAYING THAT'S OFTEN ATTRIBUTED to Yvon Chouinard: "The more you know, the less you need." Chouinard wasn't the first person to say that, but all his years of climbing and mountaineering have likely taught him that. Climbers who are less sure of their skills or the climb ahead might take way more protective gear than is necessary (I know I have). Eventually, as climbers become more confident in their skills, they will trim down the amount of gear they carry up a climb, thus making the climber lighter in weight and more efficient (and less fatigued at the top of the climb).

The same is true for hiking, backpacking, traveling to a new country, air travel, or any sort of adventure. Every new experience is a chance for you to analyze what you took with you, what you used, and what you didn't and then pare down your gear or luggage for next time.

Traveling light, in any form, can be its own luxury. Think about it: Would you rather carry a 40-pound backpack or a 30-pound backpack? Would you rather deal with a huge, unwieldy rolling suitcase on a train trip around Europe or a small bag you can easily lift into overhead baggage compartments? Simplifying your packing list can eliminate a significant amount of stress from a trip or outdoor adventure. Sure, you would love to have four pairs of shoes on your trip, but if you only brought two, you might be able to take a smaller suitcase. Same with clothes—how many outfits do you really need? Can you find a place to do laundry somewhere in the middle of your trip and cut your clothing list in half? Can you wear the same things two or three days of your trip instead of just once? Probably.

Very experienced backpackers focus on cutting weight and bulk wherever they can and often start long trips with a base backpack weight (not including food and water) of less than 10 pounds, which is incredibly light when you consider most backpacking tents often weigh 4 or 5 pounds on their own. But again, experience plus frequently analyzing what you need and what you don't need pays off—especially on the first day of that backpacking trip when hikers hoist their packs onto their shoulders for the first time and start walking under their weight. It's a far different trip to start when you feel crushed by your backpack than when it feels light.

It may not be for everyone—we all have certain creature comforts we think we can't live without. But do you need all of them on the same trip? It might be worth thinking about. Learn to live with a little less next time and a little less the next time, and so on until you're pared down to the essentials, just to see how it feels. Who knows—you might actually find that you like going "light and fast," whether it's on the trail or on a long weekend trip somewhere.

#2

Trek the Annapurna Circuit, Nepal

LENGTH: Quit Your Job

DESCRIPTION: Plenty of countries in the world have beautiful mountains—just none as big as the Himalayas. If you've ever been curious about what it's like to wander around the true giants of our planet, the 20,000-plus-foot-tall glaciated peaks with avalanches ripping down their flanks, the Annapurna Circuit might be for you.

Most trekkers take 14 to 25 days to walk the 145-mile length of the circuit, starting in either Besi Sahar or Pokhara (each town a few hours' drive from Kathmandu) and hiking to altitudes of up to 17,769 feet on their way around the Annapurna Massif. That's right, the mountain is so big, it takes weeks to walk around it. From many vantage points on the route, you'll be able to see some of the highest peaks in the world, several of them over 26,000 feet (that's 11,000 feet higher than California's Mount Whitney, for comparison).

Camping is not necessary on the Annapurna Circuit, thanks to the local network of trekker-friendly teahouses, where you'll sleep and dine on Nepalese fare like dal bhat and yak butter tea. Of course, not taking camping gear and food means one other big plus for the trek: You don't have to carry a big, heavy backpack. The route is not difficult to follow, but hiring a guide service to lead you on your trek is affordable and takes the guesswork out of reserving nights at teahouses. Several options now exist to cut down on walking mileage by driving some parts of the route—but if you're taking 2 weeks to fly halfway across the world, why not take 3 or 4?

SEASON: Year-round

INFO: nepaltrekkinginfo.com

© iStock.com/blyjak

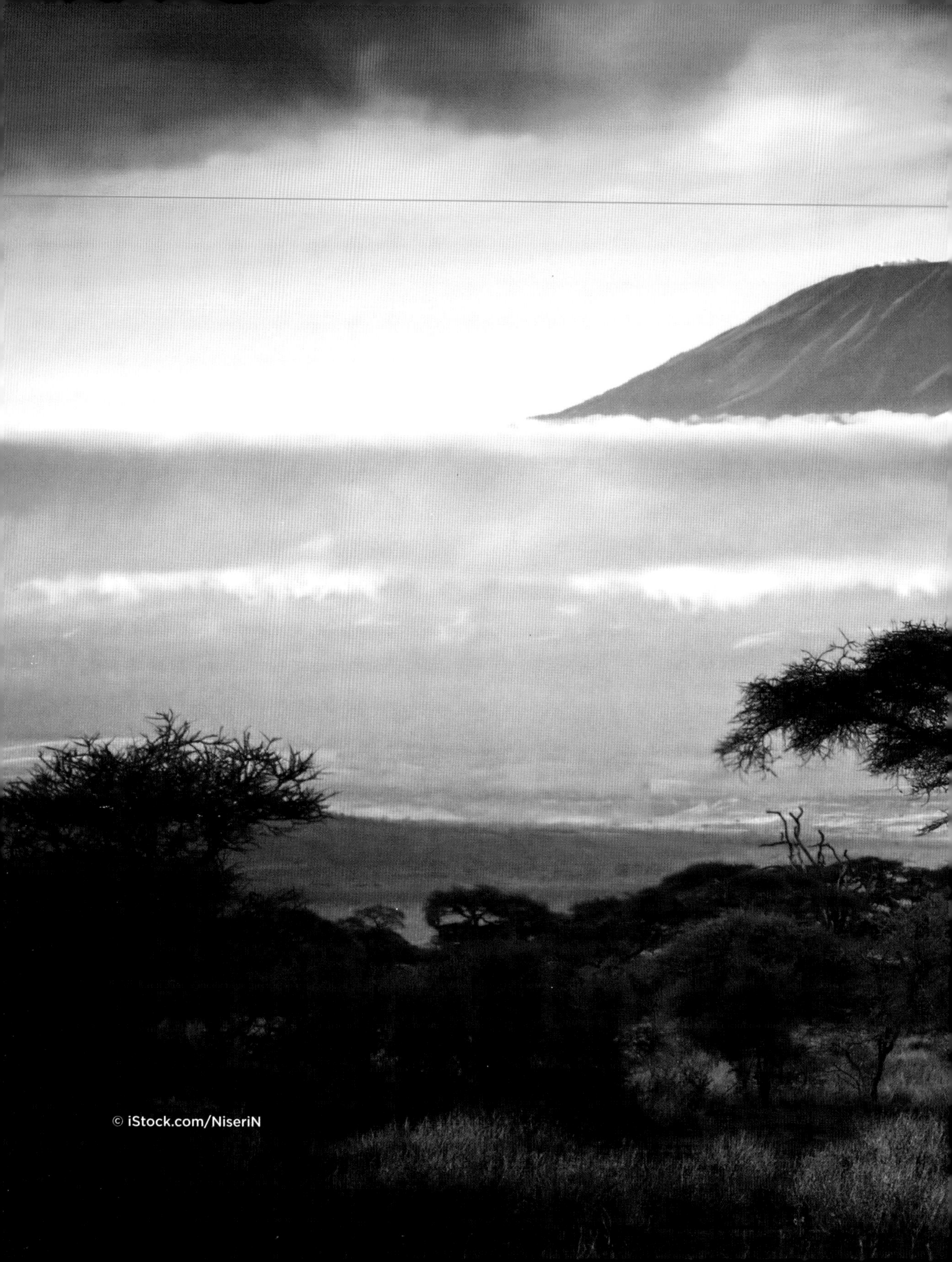

TWO-WEEKLONG ADVENTURES

TWO WEEKS: PRETTY MUCH THE MINIMUM amount of vacation a full-time employer will give anyone the first year of a job. It's perfectly reasonable to take all two weeks of that paid time off all at once, and it's also perfectly reasonable to try to squeeze the trip of a lifetime into those two weeks (although more time is always better). These trips will fit into roughly two weeks or less, including travel on either end when applicable, and they cover four different continents. This chapter should give you enough to do with two weeks of annual allotted vacation for the next six years and enough passport stamps and stories for a lifetime. Of course, you'd be fortunate to do one of them, let alone all of them. But what else are you going to do with all that vacation time? You can't take it with you.

Trek the Tour
du Mont Blanc

LENGTH: Two-Weeklong

DESCRIPTION: Mont Blanc, as the glaciated 15,781-foot-tall high point of the Alps, is a popular climb to no one's surprise. But you don't have to climb it to have an amazing mountain adventure—hundreds of outdoor enthusiasts leave the crampons at home and circumnavigate the peak, spending 11 days walking around its flanks and crossing borders into France, Switzerland, and Italy along the way.

The Tour du Mont Blanc covers 105 miles of trekking and 32,800 feet of elevation gain over 1.5 weeks. It's a stout hike, but the saving grace is you'll spend every night in a bed, either in a mountain hut (with dinner and breakfast included) up high or in a hotel or bed-and-breakfast in one of the seven valleys the route crosses. That means you don't have to carry a tent, sleeping bag, stove, pots and pans, or breakfast and dinner.

Hikers typically begin and end the trek in the village of Les Houches, France, just outside of the mountaineering mecca of Chamonix. The trek combines big hiking days with easier walks between huts—the steepest day is typically the first climb out of Les Houches, with 5,000 feet of elevation gain, and the longest day of walking is 17.5 miles. The highest point on the trek is just over 8,500 feet. Unlike some of the other long treks of Europe (like the Haute Route), you'll end right where you started, so there's no need for a shuttle.

SEASON: Mid-June–mid-Sept

INFO: autourdumontblanc.com/en

© iStock.com/Vitalalp

Don't Make a To-Do List
on Your Vacation

© iStock.com/Vitalalp

WE'VE ALL BEEN GUILTY OF THIS at one time or another: We plan a trip some-where and make a list, in our heads or on paper, of all the things we want to see or do when we're in that new, exciting place. Go to the Empire State Building, get on the Staten Island Ferry, walk through Times Square, see Central Park, go to Shake Shack or Grimaldi's, and so on. We all have things we want to check off, things we've seen on postcards or in magazines or on TV, and they're important to us.

When traveling, though, this can make things even more stressful. Have you ever had the feeling you're getting behind schedule on your vacation? That sucks. You're taking a vacation, and the whole point of that vacation was to relax, not to schedule yourself into a panic. Americans (including myself) are pretty good at this, and it's hard to step back and realize when you're doing it.

I've only recently gotten control of myself and taken steps to erase the stress from vacation. I have scheduled backpacking trips with very short mileage goals, scheduled bike tours with enough leeway in the each day's mileage to have time to sit in cafés and stop into art galleries, and left totally blank days on visits to national parks or other places to have time to just wander around aimlessly, which is not something I ever do in real life. But I'm trying.

Scheduling every hour of your trip before you go somewhere is assuming you know everything you need to know about a place before you even get there. Once you get there, you'll very likely find out that this is not the case. If you've ever been to a new place and struck up a conversation with someone else—a local or a fellow vacationer—and they recommended something you should see before you leave, you'll know there's nothing worse than finding yourself saying, "I'd love to, but we just don't have the time." The Internet is great, but it can't show you everything about a place before you get there.

You shouldn't feel bad about having a few goals or tick list items for your trips. But leave some breathing room in your schedule. Make a few loose goals you want to do by the end of your trip, and keep the freedom for improvisation. I think you'll agree that it's better to have some stories that begin with "... and one day, we were just wandering around, and we found this incredible little shop/restaurant/pub..." than it is to say, "We achieved every goal on our Official Vacation Checklist."

#1
Climb Kilimanjaro, Tanzania

LENGTH: Two-Weeklong

DESCRIPTION: Completing the "Seven Summits"—climbing the highest mountain on each continent—is a lofty, expensive, and logistically challenging goal. Mount Everest alone takes around 50 days and $50,000 to $70,000. And that's only one of the Seven Summits.

If you want to tag just one of the Seven Summits, however, Kilimanjaro, the 19,340-foot-tall high point of Africa, is probably within reach, both financially and skill level–wise. You don't need any technical mountaineering experience on Kilimanjaro, just fitness and ability to deal with altitude. The climb can be done in as little as 2 weeks, including acclimatization to the high elevation—but most folks will tell you that it's worthwhile to also schedule a safari trip to see some African megafauna while you're there. The climb alone (without the safari) can be done for around $3,000, not including airfare to and from Tanzania. One of the best things about climbing Kilimanjaro, aside from the once-in-a-lifetime experience, incredible views, and physical challenge, is that guide services are required to use local guides. So no matter which company you choose, you're employing local residents who are making a living wage.

The climb itself is all hiking and lots of it. You'll ascend more than 16,000 feet over almost 40 miles, deliberately moving up the mountain to successively higher camps over the span of a week. The peak is almost a mile higher than anything in the Lower 48, so teaching your body to deal with lower pressure and less available oxygen is the biggest challenge—hence, the time taken to gradually work up the mountain and ensure a successful summit bid to the roof of Africa.

SEASON: June–Mar

INFO: ultimatekilimanjaro.com

#12

Book Passage on Freighter Ship, United States to Europe

LENGTH: Two-Weeklong

DESCRIPTION: It's not an all-inclusive cruise ship—it's an adventure. Not that cruises can't be adventures (just ask David Foster Wallace or the Unsinkable Molly Brown), but booking a passage on a freighter is a little less, well, cushy than your standard island cruise. No one's getting paid to pamper you on a freighter, so there aren't massages and squash games and lavish meals—you're essentially a nonworking member of the ship's crew. You eat with the crew, hang out, find ways to fill your time during the day, and watch the ocean go by. You'll have your own bunk-room, and it's possible you may be able to interact with the ship's crew—but that's up to the ship's captain.

Trips from the East Coast of the United States to Europe take between 16 and 19 days and cost $100 to $150 per day that you're on the ship. There's no Wi-Fi on board most freighters, although there is a satellite phone you will pay a fee to use. Besides that, you should plan on finding ways to entertain yourself for a couple weeks—i.e., bring lots of books or a tablet with lots of books on it. If you're looking to escape for a few weeks, a freighter cruise is a relatively comfortable way to do it as opposed to, say, hiking into the Himalayas. Three meals a day, a bed at night, and watching the ocean roll by for days at a time.

Booking freighter cruises is a little more involved than buying a ticket online. You'll contact a freighter cruise company with a destination in mind (United States to Europe), and they'll let you know what they have available and when. Keep in mind, freighter ships are in business to move freight not people, and they move a very small amount of people, so don't expect to go to a travel website and book a reservation in a few clicks.

SEASON: Year-round

INFO: freightercruises.com

Nine Travel Tips to
Lower Your Stress Levels

© iStock.com/MichaelUtech

1. **NEVER PLAN FOR THE BEST-CASE SCENARIO.** Your bag is always going to take longer to get to the baggage claim than you think it will, especially if your friend or family member is circling the airport waiting for you to emerge. The line at the rental car counter will always take longer than you want it to. Traffic will always be 10 to 300 percent worse than you imagine. Adjust your schedule to the world, because the world doesn't care about your schedule.

2. **ALWAYS PEE,** especially in places like Manhattan, where public restrooms are so scarce there's an app for finding them. Yes, I know you're not 6 years old. Just go whenever you can—just before you leave the coffee shop or restaurant, just before you get on the plane. Even if you don't "have to." See, aren't you more relaxed now?

3. **CARRY A WATER BOTTLE.** Feel like shit when you got off the plane? There's a good chance you're dehydrated. Flight attendants dispense water in 8-ounce doses (and you probably ordered a gin and tonic or a coffee instead of water anyway). Bring your own water bottle, and experience the joy of not relying on other people or retailers for your hydration.

4. **GET TO THE AIRPORT EARLY.** Once you leave your house (or hotel), lots of things are out of your control: traffic, parking, ticketing lines, TSA lines, the person in front of you who can't get their smartphone code to scan. You can't control those things, but you can give yourself enough time so that each one of them doesn't cause a 20 percent increase in your blood pressure. Yes, the coffee in the airport isn't usually that great, but I'd rather be through security drinking a halfway decent coffee and knowing I'll make my flight than be 30 minutes away from the airport drinking a great cup of coffee.

5. **GET AISLE SEATS.** Let's be honest, there are no "good seats" in economy class anymore, are there? I was a late adopter of this one. Yes, there's no view, but unlike window seats and middle seats, you at least have space to lean into if you're sitting next to an armrest hoarder or manspreader. Plus, you can get up to use the restroom anytime you want without bothering anyone. (See #2.)

6. **USE CURBSIDE CHECK-IN.** For a few dollars' tip, you can usually skip lines and ditch your checked bag way more quickly than you can inside the airport.

7. **GET AN AIRLINE CREDIT CARD.** For a small annual fee, you can often get a free checked bag (eliminate anxiety about overhead compartment space, plus you don't have to drag your bag with you through the airport/airports) and priority boarding. Plus, you might earn enough miles to get a free trip home to see your mom (or a free flight to Europe).

8. **DON'T PACK A BUNCH OF SHIT YOU DON'T NEED.** Just like in backpacking and mountaineering, the weight and volume of your belongings can have an inverse effect on your ability to experience joy. Be mindful of this when you pack, and leave a couple things at home.

9. **RELAX.** Put Miles Davis's *Kind of Blue* or John Coltrane's *Blue Train* on your phone, bring headphones, and listen to it as you take your time cruising through the airport and enjoy not worrying if you'll make it to your gate on time.

Ski the Haute Route, France/Switzerland

LENGTH: Two-Weeklong

DESCRIPTION: It's probably the most famous multiday ski tour in the world, a 7-day traverse between the mountaineering capitals of Chamonix, France, at the foot of Mont Blanc, to Zermatt, Switzerland, at the foot of the Matterhorn. Every day, you ski across glacial valleys and glaciers between the enormous jagged peaks of the Alps. Every night, you sleep in a mountain hut perched in sometimes unbelievable locations. With meals and shelter provided, you can ski every day with only a light backpack, carrying your lunch, water, clothing, and a sleeping bag liner—oh, and maybe a toothbrush.

Although strikingly beautiful, the Alps also command respect—weather is very dynamic, and it's easy to get lost in a whiteout. For this reason and for ease in taking care of the logistics of making reservations at multiple mountain huts, many skiers who tackle the Haute Route choose to use a guide service. Skiing with a mountain guide provides you with someone who has skied the route many times in variable conditions and has a passion for the experience. Depending on the size of your guided group, costs per skier can be as low as $3,000 for the trip (not including travel to and from Europe), which is substantial, but plenty of people spend that much money on the lodging for a weeklong ski trip in the United States. If you want to see the best of the snow-covered Alps and understand the feeling of skiing past the Matterhorn into picture-book Zermatt, it's a pretty solid deal.

SEASON: Mar–Apr

INFO: cosleyhouston.com

Gavin Woody

Climb Mount Vinson, Antarctica

LENGTH: Two-Weeklong

DESCRIPTION: Although Mount Everest is probably the most famous guided mountain climb in the world, some might argue that Antarctica's Mount Vinson is just as big of an adventure with way less time commitment, a lower cost, and more oxygen. At 16,067 feet and far below the Antarctic Circle, Mount Vinson is no walk in the park, but it takes only 16 to 20 days, depending on weather and conditions. With a guide (recommended), costs are around $40,000, including everything but flights to Punta Arenas, Chile.

After flying to Punta Arenas (and a day checking gear and repacking), you'll get on a flight to Antarctica, where you'll transfer to a smaller plane to fly to Vinson Base Camp at 7,000 feet. For a week, you'll carry loads to higher camps on the mountain, setting yourself up for a summit bid when weather permits.

Vinson isn't the most popular of the Seven Summits for obvious reasons (it's cold, it's in Antarctica, and so on), but it's a true mountaineering adventure. Guided climbers are required to have significant mountaineering experience and know how to handle crampons, an ice axe, and roped travel in order to make a successful bid to the top of the highest peak on the bottom of the world.

SEASON: Dec–Jan

INFO: mountainguides.com

flickr.com/Christopher Michel

Showering Every Day
Is a Waste of Time

© iStock.com/emicristea

IF I COULD GIVE EVERY TRAVELER ONE PIECE OF ADVICE on how to get more out of their vacation time, it would be this: Lower your personal hygiene standards. More specifically, learn to go a few days without a shower.

Before you scrunch up your face and tell me how disgusting that is, let's think about this: Not so long ago, we weren't showering every day before we went into work mostly because showers didn't exist. In fact, someone a couple branches up your family tree probably bathed in the same bathwater as the rest of the family once every few weeks or once every month.

Now, I'm not asking you to reuse bathwater (which, let's be honest, is actually pretty gross). I'm saying step back and consider why you shower every day. It's probably because you work in an office and have to look and smell "presentable." Fair enough. Why are you on vacation? To get away from work and everything that requires: business casual, meetings, sitting at a desk for 8 or 9 hours, answering e-mails, eating at your desk.

While you're getting away from work, how about you also get away from that pressure to look and smell "presentable"? If you're on a good old-fashioned camping road trip, showering is a real pain: You have to dig out new clothes, find your toiletries, find a place to shower, and then shower, dry off, and put all your stuff back. That's a half hour or more that you could have been spending doing something else, including but not limited to: sitting by a campfire, dozing in a hammock, sitting in a chair drinking a beer and watching the sun go down, reading a book, napping, or going for a walk.

You probably don't smell as bad as you might imagine you do when you're on vacation, especially if you're in nature. Sure, you don't smell like shampoo, conditioner, soap, deodorant, perfume/cologne, and laundry detergent, but you're not walking into a meeting with senior management on your vacation, are you? That's right, you're sitting in a hammock or building a campfire. And when you get back to your job, you'll miss that campfire smell on your clothes.

On vacation, the best use of your time does not include making yourself adhere to your normal grooming routine. If the friends you're on vacation with express disdain that you put your hair in a ponytail under a baseball cap instead of blow-drying and styling it for 4 days, you need new friends. I've spent 10 days in a tent with friends on multiple occasions, and where we were going, showering was not an option. And we're still friends to this day.

There are a few ways to keep yourself moderately clean, and they don't take nearly as much time as showering. Get a small bottle of travel soap to wash your face with and a box of wet wipes to maintain other areas. Use as necessary. If you walk into a coffee shop and people shake their heads and pinch their noses as you walk past, consider showering. But it probably won't get that far.

Trek Torres del Paine, Patagonia

LENGTH: Two-Weeklong

DESCRIPTION: The W Trek is one of the most sought-after backpacking trips in the world for many reasons, not the least of which are the dreamlike sculpted spires and peaks that line the horizons of the valleys of Torres del Paine. There are also the glaciers, the ice-blue lakes, and the accessibility—it's a 43-mile, 5-day, 4-night backpacking trip, starting and ending with a bus ride to/from the city of Puerto Natales. It's called the "W Trek" because, on a map, the route forms a W, the legs of which end in unforgettable views of the Grey Glacier, the French Valley, and the famous Paine Towers.

  The trek is straightforward and doable by anyone with a decent amount of backpacking experience, but it's also possible to do the hike with a guide service, sleep in a dormitory bed every night, have a prepared box lunch to take with you every day, take a more relaxed pace, and spend a week on the route. A typical guide service costs $1,400–1,900 per person for the entire trek, food and lodging included. But of course, if you choose to guide yourself, backpack, and sleep in a tent every night, the cost is much lower—about $110, which leaves you plenty of money to get a celebratory meal back in Puerto Natales on your last day.

SEASON: Dec–Feb

INFO: adventurealan.com

Chris Shane

WEEKLONG ADVENTURES

WITH A WEEK, YOU CAN SEE A LOT OF A COUNTRY— even one as big as the United States, as two of the trips in this chapter prove. You can take an Amtrak train across the US, drive the entire Pacific Coast, climb Mount Rainier or El Capitan, or trek somewhere like Machu Picchu or the Routeburn Track in New Zealand. Not all of these adventures take seven days to complete—some are three or four days out in the field. That doesn't seem like a huge time commitment for a memory of a lifetime, like standing on top of Rainier or hanging off the side of El Capitan, but it really is all you need. Caveat: You also need to train a lot for things like climbing Mount Rainier or El Capitan. But you don't need to train at all to drive the Pacific Coast or ride an Amtrak train from New York to Los Angeles.

Ride Amtrak from Coast to Coast

LENGTH: Weeklong

DESCRIPTION: It's no Trans-Siberian Railroad, but it might be one of the easiest ways to see the United States from Pacific to Atlantic: Riding a train with a sleeper car from coast to coast takes less than 4 days. Sound like a lot? If you hopped in a car in New York and drove 8 hours a day, it would take you 5.5 days to get to San Francisco. Of course, a direct flight is way faster, but that's not the point.

Unless you live on one of the coasts, though, you will have to fly to your starting point and home from your end point, so keep that in mind when planning. Amtrak trains start in Los Angeles and San Diego on the West Coast, if you absolutely have to start in a city that touches the ocean. If not, you can start in Portland, Oregon; Seattle, Washington; Vancouver, B.C., or Emeryville, California (outside San Francisco). On the East Coast, you can start in Miami, Florida; Newport News, Virginia; New York; Boston, Massachusetts; and Portland, Maine. Costs vary according to your route, but if you have a travel partner and share your sleeper car room, it's cheaper. All meals are included while you're on the train (you'll eat in the dining car for breakfast, lunch, and dinner).

You will have (or be able to schedule) layovers in different cities along your route, so plan accordingly if you'd like some time to explore. One thing to consider: When traveling west to east, set your watch back an hour every time you change time zones. Because of the speed of travel, you'll only cross into one new time zone each day, so it can be a bit like "falling back" during Daylight Saving Time. If traveling from east to west, you're "gaining an hour" every time you switch time zones on the train.

SEASON: Any season

INFO: amtrak.com

12 All-Purpose
Adventure Gear Items

Jessica Kelley

IT'S EASY TO WALK INTO A GEAR STORE and be completely bewildered by all the stuff on the walls or wonder if you should just buy everything they have so you can get started doing things in the outdoors. Calm down. You don't need to buy everything. If you want to get started doing things in the outdoors but don't know where to begin buying gear, here are a few things I'd put on my shopping list if I were starting all over again at zero gear. Hopefully, it will help you sort through all that stuff in the gear store and guide you to what you really need to get started. Obviously, gear companies would love to have you buy everything they sell, but truthfully, a good foundation of stuff can get you going on plenty of adventures. Lots of these things can be found used on eBay or at gear consignment shops.

1. **30-LITER BACKPACK.** A 30-liter pack is a good size for lots of single-day activities—day hikes, ski resort days, peak bagging, hauling books/laptops to the office or across campus, bike commuting, picnicking, whatever. If you're buying one back-pack for all your one-day activities, 30 liters is a great size. A bajillion people make 30-liter packs (or 28-liter or 32-liter), and you can find them all over the Internet.

2. **LIGHTWEIGHT SOFT-SHELL JACKET.** A solid lightweight, breathable, soft-shell jacket should be a go-to layer for spring and summer (or higher-altitude) moun-tain bike rides, trail runs, multipitch rock climbs, peak bagging, day hikes, or anything where you might get a stiff, cool breeze when you're a little sweaty or exposed to some wind and possibly a little rain.

3. **60-LITER BACKPACK.** A 60-liter pack isn't the biggest you can buy, but most of us aren't going on backpacking trips longer than 7 days often enough to justify own-ing anything much bigger than that. I think 60 liters is perfect for 3-day or 4-day trips when you want to pack heavy, multiday climbs of peaks like Mount Shasta or Mount Rainier, as a piece of checked luggage for most things I do (which don't often—actually, ever—involve clothes on hangers), 7-day backpacking trips when you don't want to be carrying a bunch of extra crap anyway, and days of extreme luxury at the climbing crag. You should get a pack that fits you first and worry about features later (in my opinion).

4. **HEADLAMP.** If you go camping, backpacking, need to find things under your fridge, do car repairs on the street in front of your apartment, have permanently shut off your car's interior light because of your tendency to leave it on and find a dead battery the next time you try to start your car, a headlamp is for you. You can spend $400 on one that will illuminate a mountain bike trail at 20 mph (useful for those times you find yourself needing lighting while traveling at high speeds), or you can spend $19.95 and get a basic one (useful for everything but lighting while trav-eling at high speeds). I've always preferred simple, minimalist lights that run on small batteries and don't light up a million yards away from you or have a bunch of functions that you have to tap Morse codes on the power button to operate. I never leave the trailhead without a headlamp stuffed in my pack somewhere, and that's prevented a few nights of sitting on a rock in the dark waiting for the sun to come up again.

5. **WATER BOTTLES.** To paraphrase Ian MacKaye, companies are not selling you water; they're selling you a plastic bottle. Water is free. If you have a water bottle, you can access and store water so you can take it with you when you walk away from the source, such as an airport drinking fountain. With a full water bottle or two, you have some chance of actually staying hydrated on a trans-Atlantic flight, since you don't have to rely on flight attendants pouring you a 4-ounce cup of bottled water every 3 hours.

6. **TRAIL RUNNING SHOES.** Something they don't tell you about running shoes: You can just walk in them if you don't want to run. In fact, it's often less strenuous than running. You can wear trail running shoes for hiking and backpacking, as long as you can live without the ankle support and stout outsole of hiking boots. You can also use trail running shoes to run on surfaces other than trails. I wouldn't stop anyone from buying a pair of hiking boots, but if you have room for only one pair of outdoor shoes in your luggage, trail running shoes are probably more versatile.

7. **RAIN SHELL.** If you go out there, you're going to get rained on sometime. There are tons of different models available, and generally, the more expensive they are, the more breathable they are (that money is spent on the technology in the jacket, and everyone's trying to make a lightweight, breathable, waterproof jacket). Get something that says "waterproof" that's in your price range, and you'll be happy. If you'd like a super-packable ultralight one to take for "just in case" showers, there are plenty of those available in the $125–150 range.

8. **PUFFY JACKET.** Pros: super-warm, compresses down to nothing in your backpack, can be used as a pillow. Cons: rips easily, doesn't insulate when wet (unless it's synthetic insulation or treated down), easily perforated by flying sparks from campfires. Be good to your puffy jacket and it will be good to you. It's like an appetizer for the later, full meal of getting into your sleeping bag. It can be your happy place. I have always used small amounts of Krazy Glue to patch the little holes in my puffy jackets, but most people use duct tape.

9. **TWO-PERSON BACKPACKING TENT.** If you want to buy a bunch of tents for all your needs, you could get a one-person tent for all your solo backpacking (or bikepacking) trips, a two-person tent for trips you take with a friend, a big car-camping

tent for weekends when you go out with friends and want to spread out all your stuff and maybe just stand up inside your tent because you can. Or you could just buy a basic two-person backpacking tent and use it for everything—including not taking up as much space as three separate tents in your gear closet/garage.

10. 15°F SLEEPING BAG. I've done most of my camping and backpacking in the past decade in the mountains and desert of the West, and I've never found a 15°F sleeping bag to be overkill. Only in rare, way-late-season situations has it proven to be too chilly. If you're a very cold sleeper or are planning on winter camping, a bag with a rating closer to 0°F is probably more appropriate, but I would say most people buy something moderate (15°F or 20°F rating) and then buy a different sleeping bag for winter so they're not hauling around the extra weight of a winter bag all year. A 15°F or 20°F sleeping bag is a great all-purpose, three-season sleeping bag. Down sleeping bags are more compressible and lighter but generally more expensive, and synthetic bags are bulkier but have traditionally held insulative value better when wet. Lots of companies are now using treated down, which has helped down insulate better when wet (and dry more quickly than untreated down). I haven't had a ton of experiences where my sleeping bag has been completely saturated, but I have been very impressed with treated down in situations of extreme condensation (sleeping without a tent next to a river or another humid scenario) and picking up moisture from the inside of a wet tent or from wet clothes and gear during a rainy trip.

11. SLEEPING PAD. These pads are for sleeping on the ground. They're not all the same, but they're all better than sleeping on the actual ground. I can't 100 percent recommend one particular model for super-cushy unpuncturable comfort, but I've never carried one that weighs more than 1.5 pounds.

12. ISOBUTANE (CANISTER FUEL) STOVE. Yes, Jetboils are exciting, efficient, and compact, but I think a solid (non-Jetboil) canister stove is a great entry point for anyone who's getting started in the outdoors. I like Jetboils for certain applications, but cooking nondehydrated meals in a pot is not one of them. If you want to make your own pasta, grab a simple canister stove and a windscreen (if it doesn't come with one, make one out of a foil turkey roasting pan from the grocery store) and get going.

Climb Mount Rainier, Washington

LENGTH: Weeklong

DESCRIPTION: Guides and climbers who have spent time on the mountain will tell you Mount Rainier has everything a big mountain in Asia has—glacier, crevasses, seracs, and intense weather. But, you'll probably notice that it's a lot easier to get to than, say, Ama Dablam.

Rainier is visible from the city of Seattle on clear days, and even a guided ascent is a quick trip most people can fit into their schedules: 3.5 days total, including 1 day of learning how to walk in crampons, use an ice axe, and be an efficient member of a rope team. The climb of the trade route on the peak, Disappointment Cleaver, involves 9,000 vertical feet of snow climbing, broken into 2 days: On Day 1, climbers walk up the Muir Snowfield from the Paradise parking lot at 5,400 feet to Camp Muir, 10,188 feet. After going to bed early and spending a short night at Camp Muir, climbers leave the hut (or tents) at 1 or 2 a.m. on Day 2 to begin the summit day, a climb from Camp Muir to the 14,410-foot summit.

It's a short time commitment, but a huge fitness test—there's nothing that quite compares to hiking up steep inclines for that long on snow. But, with the right preparation (becoming good friends with the Stairmaster, doing lunges, or running/walking flights of stairs) and a sizable amount of mental fortitude, it's doable with very little mountaineering experience.

SEASON: June–Sept

INFO: rmiguides.com

Jessica Kelley

Chris Shane

#13

Traverse the Presidential Range, New Hampshire (in Winter)

LENGTH: Weeklong

DESCRIPTION: New Hampshire's Mount Washington is well known for having "the worst weather in the world." It sits at the convergence of three storm paths, has seen wind speeds measuring up to 231 mph, and has had winter temperatures as low as –115°F. So it's a great place to head for a winter hike, right?

If you're looking for a full-on mountain adventure on the East Coast, a winter Presidential traverse is it. But it's not to be taken lightly. It's a 22-mile hike often necessitating snowshoes and crampons, covering 8,500 feet of elevation gain and at least 2 nights of camping out in cold conditions (most parties take 3 to 5 days to complete it during the winter). Sound like fun? There's a reason it's a mountaineering rite of passage in the Northeast: It's tough.

After the first summit—Mount Madison—you've knocked out most of the elevation gain, but you're then exposed to the elements on the high ridge for almost 12 miles. If you're lucky (or just get a good weather forecast), you won't get the high winds and freezing windchill the Presidential Range is famous for in winter, and you'll tag the other seven Presidential summits without incident: Mounts Adams, Jefferson, Clay, Washington, Monroe, Eisenhower, and Pierce.

If a winter traverse isn't your thing, a summer hike across the range is also a great way to see the range and doable in as little as a day (if you're extremely fit and efficient). The weather can still change in an instant and be dangerous during the summer, so be prepared.

SEASON: Dec–Mar

INFO: mountainsenseguides.com

The Benefits of Going
in the Off-Season

Chris Shane

"NOTHING DRAWS A CROWD LIKE A CROWD," goes the saying. We've all been there—sitting in traffic in a national park or sharing a famous photo destination with 200 of our closest friends, simultaneously thinking, "This place would be so great if it weren't for all the people," and, "I'm one of those 200 people."

So how do you beat the crowds? One way is to go in the off-season. Every great place has a few months a year that are the most popular. If you want to see and be seen, by all means, go skiing over the Christmas holiday, go to Yosemite in the middle of the summer, and travel in the Alps in August (when most Europeans take their month-long holiday).

But if you'd rather not share someplace with "the crowds," do a little research—when are the busy times? Is the weather still okay a few weeks before or after the high tourist season? Is there an open-and-shut case for not going to that place during the off-season, or do the pros still outweigh the cons?

It will pay off. You'll make some sacrifices, whether it's a less-predictable weather forecast, fewer restaurants open, or fewer lodging options. But it can be more affordable (plane tickets, hotels, and campgrounds costing less because of less demand), less crowded, and maybe more enjoyable.

For example, the desert Southwest, especially Moab, can be extremely busy during "Spring Break," which seems to take up the entire month of March nowadays. Fall, especially October, can also be very busy. So what to do? How about the 4 weeks between November 15 and December 15? Yes, it's cold at night, and the days are short, but there's a lot you can accomplish between 8 a.m. and 5 p.m., especially when you're not fighting thousands of other people for parking spots, backpacking permits, restaurant tables, and hotel rooms.

Lots of traffic to US national parks is families with children, and parents, of course, schedule their vacations during their kids' summer break from classes. If you don't have kids, it makes sense to plan your vacations to hot spots like Yellowstone National Park just after students go back to school in the early fall, when reservations are much easier to make.

I've been to Ireland in January, the Grand Canyon in December, and Telluride in May (after ski season ends and before most of the trails are dry from spring runoff). Every experience was made a little better just by the fact that we felt like we had the whole place to ourselves—even if a lot of the "tourist amenities" were closed for the off-season, and it was a little cold or a little rainy.

Of course, lots of places are popular at certain times for a reason, and it's not a bad thing to be in those places during popular times—riding the mountain bike trails around Moab when it's sunny and 72°F, for example. But if you go, be prepared to be patient and meet some new friends from all over the world.

19

Climb El Capitan, Yosemite, California

LENGTH: Weeklong

DESCRIPTION: It's the most famous rock wall in the world—a 3,000-foot-high sea of granite towering above the Yosemite Valley. Climbing it is on thousands of climbers' life lists, and many never make it to the valley to attempt it. Those who do usually spend several days working their way up the wall, hauling everything they need with them—which includes climbing gear, camping gear, food, human waste (eww), and water (because there's no water on El Cap unless it rains, and you don't want it to rain up there).

And you don't spend all your time just climbing up there. Ascents of El Cap involve long hours belaying, putting together and taking apart portaledges (those human-sized trays that attach to the wall to give climbers a flat surface to sleep on) every evening and morning, and managing life in a vertical environment (i.e., don't drop anything). But the climbing is magnificent and plentiful. No matter what route you choose to climb to the top of El Cap, you're climbing somewhere between 1,800 and 3,000 feet of some of the best granite in America (if not the world).

Only one company, Yosemite Mountaineering School & Guide Service, guides climbs of El Capitan, and if you're interested, it'll cost you $5,800 for a 6-day climb. But where else can you spend a week climbing granite without touching the ground?

SEASON: Apr–Oct

INFO: travelyosemite.com/things-to-do/rock-climbing

20

Mountain Bike the White Rim Trail, Utah

LENGTH: Weeklong

DESCRIPTION: This is an epic mountain bike tour without carrying epic amounts of gear. That's right, the preferred protocol for the 100-mile White Rim Trail through the Islands in the Sky District of Canyonlands National Park is to ride with Jeep (or truck) support and to take 3 to 4 days to do it. What does that mean for the mountain bikers? As much water as your support vehicle can carry, for one thing—and that means a lot on the White Rim, where there are no water sources. It also means you can take all kinds of heavy food and camping gear and a cooler full of beer if you want.

A vehicle to carry all your stuff is wonderful, but so is the scenery and the riding on the White Rim. It's so named because of the layer of White Rim sandstone that forms the top of the cliffs above the Green River and Colorado River, where the road takes riders, weaving through a wonderland of red sandstone cliffs and geological formations. Riding is all on a four-wheel-drive road, so it's not technical, but you ride about 1,000 vertical feet down to the road from above on your first day, so you have to pedal up that distance on your last day as well. Self-organized trips have to obtain camping permits through Canyonlands National Park. If you prefer a guide to handle logistics and permits, guided trips are available for about $900 per person.

SEASON: Sept–Oct, Mar–May

INFO: westernspirit.com

NPS/Neal Herbert

The Terrifying and Wonderful Concept of Going Without Data for a Week

© iStock.com/miksov

HERE'S A SITUATION YOU'LL FIND YOURSELF IN when going "off the grid" for a few days in the 21st century: You're on your way to the place you're going that doesn't have cell phone service, whether it's in the backcountry of Utah or Montana or the mountains in Nepal. You're getting closer to the trailhead or getting ready for takeoff on an international flight, and you're trying to catch up on those last bits of data that are coming through the Internet to you: one more check of Facebook, Insta-gram, and/or Twitter just to see if anything interesting has popped up in the past few minutes. One more check of your e-mail, even though you turned on your out-of-office autoresponder hours ago and anyone who matters already knows you're going to be gone and not communicating for a few days or a couple weeks. One more text message to really close friends or family saying, "Talk to you when I get back!"

And then it happens, the moment we all secretly dread: We're cut off from data for a few days or weeks. What if something happens? What if someone from work needs my expertise or opinion on something? What if one of the many people I follow on various social media platforms does something they've never done before? WHAT IF I MISS SOMETHING?

This feeling of anxiety may last a few minutes to a few hours until you reach that point of no return: You choose not to connect to the in-flight Wi-Fi because it's so expensive, or you chose long ago to not activate your phone in whatever country you're going to, or you're so far in the backcountry that there's no cell phone reception. Maybe you even check, just once, turning your phone off airplane mode, just to be sure there isn't some 3G/LTE creeping through the mountains or canyon walls that will allow you to look at your Instagram feed. Or maybe you don't at all.

After a day or two or three, you may notice something: that anxiety disappears and you don't care that you don't have data anymore. You focus on the things immediately in front of you, your experience on your trip, and taking photos of all the cool stuff you're seeing. Maybe you brought a book, and you sit down to read that and realize you've forgotten how nice it is.

This feeling will last until near the end of your trip, when you start to feel a tinge of excitement: You will have access to data in a few hours. You can text, call, or e-mail loved ones to let them know your trip was fun and you are okay, maybe send a couple photos.

Maybe you dive right back into everything the moment you turn on your phone, frantically responding to e-mails and texts, scrolling through all the social media things that happened while you were offline. Or maybe you don't do that, and you just let people know you're alright before putting your phone back on airplane mode and enjoying the rest of your trip, finishing your book, or just absorbing all the great things about the place you've traveled to, and telling yourself it's fine because you don't have to be back in the office until Monday, and you'll deal with all that stuff later.

Trek to Machu Picchu, Peru

LENGTH: Weeklong

DESCRIPTION: Since the "discovery" of the "Lost City of the Incas" in 1911, thousands of hikers have made the 4-day trek along the Inca Trail to the ruins of a city on the high saddle between the mountains of Machu Picchu and Huayna Picchu. The position of the city kept it safe from Spanish conquistadors, which also means it has incredible views looking into the valleys on the east and west. The architecture is pretty impressive as well: No one knows how the Inca people were able to move the large stones that make up the structures in the city that was home to an estimated 1,000 people in the 1400s and 1500s.

  If you want to trek through the mountains to get to the famous view of Machu Picchu the same way the Inca people did, it'll take 4 days and 3 nights. It's not a particularly difficult hike, but it is 26 miles and at a fairly high altitude: The trail starts at about 8,500 feet in elevation and climbs to 13,780 feet at its highest point (Machu Picchu itself is at 7,972 feet). Don't expect solitude: The trail is limited to 500 people per day, and permits are scooped up fast by trekkers from all over the world, so plan your trip well in advance.

SEASON: May–Sept

INFO: machupicchutrek.net

Drive the Pacific Coast, USA

LENGTH: Weeklong

DESCRIPTION: Fact: You can drive from Seattle, Washington, to San Diego, California, very efficiently on the inland I-5. Also a fact: You can take a week to drive from Seattle to San Diego on US 101 and SR 1, hugging the curves of the Pacific Coast and taking two-lane highways almost the entire way. If you decide to do that (highly recommended), give yourself a week or more to get it done. It's about 1,600 miles, and if you drive 5 hours a day, not including stops for coffee, bathroom breaks, and lunch, it'll take you almost exactly a week. If you want to stop anywhere cool, for example, to walk the beach in Olympic National Park in Washington, or check out the sea stacks in Cannon Beach, Oregon, or stare up at enormous trees 15 feet in diameter in Redwood National Park in California, or hike in Point Reyes National Seashore or in Muir Woods, or do anything in San Francisco or Los Angeles or San Diego . . . well, you get the point.

   The two highways that transect the Pacific Coast combine for one of the most scenic drives in the entire country, with cliffs, beaches, dunes, and old-growth forests lining the road. You could take a month to explore everything along the route if you stopped often enough and had enough time to do it, but a week or so is the perfect amount of time for some car-based sightseeing. You'll notice the coastal culture change as you drive south (or north) through three states, between urban and rural, from the sleepy coast towns of southern Oregon to the chaos of Los Angeles, and best of all, you don't need a guide or any special skills to do it.

SEASON: Any season, but summer is best in Oregon and Washington

INFO: roadtripusa.com/pacific-coast

Eight Things to Always Have in Your Backpack

© iStock.com/PytyCzech

EVEN IF YOU'RE JUST GOING OUT FOR A SHORT DAY HIKE, lots of things can happen: a sprained ankle miles from the car, running out of water, running out of daylight, a shoe falling apart. Here are a few things I always carry with me, no matter what I'm doing, whether it's a 5-mile hike or a 10-day backpacking trip.

- HEADLAMP. Have you ever hiked in the dark with no stars or moonlight? It's an adventure for sure. I had a hell of a time finding my way back to the trailhead in the dark because the hike went longer than I thought it would twice in the span of about a month back in 2004. Guess what? It's never happened again. I always take a compact, lightweight headlamp with me, no matter what I'm doing.

- SPACE BLANKET. This is a small package that looks like a fistful of aluminum foil, but it unfolds into a makeshift blanket that's big enough to wrap a human being in like a giant burrito. What good is that? Well, it reflects your body heat back onto you and can help you survive an unplanned night out. Hopefully, you'll never have to use it, but it's 3 ounces of insurance that gives me peace of mind.

- DUCT TAPE. Everyone knows of the magical properties of duct tape, but you don't have to take the whole roll with you in the backcountry. Just make a smaller roll of about 15 feet of tape (should be about 1 inch in diameter when you're done), and throw that in your backpack. If the sole rips off your shoe, you'll be happy you had that duct tape to fix it. Also good for blisters.

- BALING WIRE. A small amount of baling wire can be a lifesaver if you break a snowshoe in the backcountry, and it can repair lots of other things with a little imagination.

- PARACHUTE CORD. Fix a broken shoelace, rig a guyline on a tent, restrap a backpack shoulder strap, etc. Again, you don't need 100 feet of it—but 15–20 feet is great.

- IODINE TABLETS. A small jar of iodine tablets weighs 3 ounces and can purify up to 25 liters of water. Why not have one with you at all times? That's enough iodine to keep you pretty well hydrated for almost a week if something bad happens and you're waiting for a rescue.

- LIGHTER. Yes, survivalists can start fires with no source of ignition. I can't. I take a lighter, which takes 1 second to light.

- MULTITOOL. Doesn't have to be expensive, doesn't have to have a million tools on it. Mostly I end up cutting cheese with it, and sometimes doing the occasional repair.

Hike the Routeburn Track, New Zealand

LENGTH: Weeklong

DESCRIPTION: There's a reason the Routeburn Track is on almost every list of "best backpacking trips in the world": pure mountain scenery—alpine valleys at your feet and striking, glaciated peaks above. That scenery is packed into a short trip: Most hikers take 3 days and 2 nights to cover the 32-km trail (that's just under 20 miles, so not even 7 miles per day). Also, you're not sleeping in a tent every night—camping is allowed, but hikers typically stay in Department of Conservation huts along the route. Okay, that's actually three reasons. Regardless, if you need a reason to visit New Zealand, the Routeburn Track is as good as any.

With its short distance and challenging but moderate elevation gain, the Routeburn Track is within reach of anyone with good fitness and some hiking experience—you won't be labeling it a "death march" for sure. The biggest challenge of the trek might be securing reservations in high season (Nov–Apr), when bookings are required for huts and camp-sites along the track. There are four huts and two campsites, and book-ings for both fill up months in advance, so plan early. The Department of Conservation huts all have bunks, mattresses, heating, toilets, gas cook-tops, solar-powered lighting, and cold running water, but you'll have to bring your own food to cook, cooking utensils, and sleeping bag.

It is possible to do the Routeburn Track outside of the high season, but flood and avalanche risks exist, huts are not staffed, and bridges may be out (and, obviously, it can be much colder!).

SEASON: Nov–Apr

INFO: doc.govt.nz/routeburntrack

© iStock.com/irisphoto2

Kayak Tour the San Juan Islands, Washington

LENGTH: Weeklong

DESCRIPTION: Imagine backpacking for 5 days, carrying everything you need with you, traversing a beautiful landscape, and sleeping under the stars every night. Okay, now imagine taking all that stuff out of your backpack, taking that heavy load off your shoulders and hips, putting it all in a lightweight boat, and instead of walking around that landscape, paddling that boat and gliding through water for 5 days.

   Sold? Well, how about if we throw in some whale watching? Kayak touring is wonderful anywhere, but Washington's San Juan Islands, the archipelago just north of Seattle, are one of the most famous sea kayaking destinations, and for good reason. Actually, there are a number of good reasons, including stable weather during the summer, forested beaches, the highest concentration of bald eagles in the Lower 48, sea otters, and, oh, no roads on any of the islands so no cars, thus, you can easily find solitude. And orcas (as previously mentioned) that you can view from water level.

   Every day, you'll paddle somewhere new, and every night, you'll sleep somewhere else, making for a grand tour of one of the most interesting coastal ecosystems in North America. It's a week of powering your own cruise ship—with way fewer people on board.

SEASON: May–Oct

INFO: sea-quest-kayak.com

Jason Zabriskie

Skip Going Out for Dinner Once a Week for a Year and Do a Grand Canyon Trip

© iStock.com/Nikolas_jkd

ONE OF THE MAIN REASONS WE CITE for not traveling more is that we just don't have the money. Traveling is expensive, and we just can't seem to get ahead enough to make it work.

To borrow a tactic out of my friend Alastair Humphreys's book *Grand Adventures*, saving a little bit of money per week can add up to a fantastic trip once a year. I know everyone knows how to do math, but I also know a lot of us avoid it because we don't like hearing the truth.

If you go out for a nice dinner once a week, you're probably (conservatively) spending $25 just on yourself, including one entrée, a drink, and a tip. That's $1,300 a year, or about what you might spend on a guided 3-day whitewater rafting trip through the Gates of Lodore in Colorado and Utah, including your flights.

Do you go through a bottle of wine or two every week at home? No, I'm not saying you have a problem, but one glass of not-that-expensive wine per evening adds up. One bottle of wine contains about six glasses of wine (and that's if you pour exactly 5-ounce glasses), and one of those per night adds up to 60 bottles of wine per year. That's $900 per year you're spending on wine—if you only have one glass of wine every night (be honest)—which is about the cost of a round-trip flight from Chicago to Iceland.

If you take a coffee break from your office, grab a latte from the nearest coffee shop, and give the barista a decent tip, you're spending $5 a day on coffee—or over the course of a work year, $1,250 on coffee, which is definitely enough to buy yourself a flight to Portland, a rental car, and a guided climb up Mount Hood.

Going out to dinner, drinking wine (or beer), and having coffee are all fun things. It all depends on what kind of fun you want to have in your life—if you want more adventure, sometimes the solution is less wine, or coffee, or that pasta dish you like at the Italian place near your apartment. But it can pay off with a summit sunrise on Mount Hood or getting splashed by the rapids in the Green River as you paddle through desert canyons.

WEEKEND-LONG ADVENTURES

NOT EVERYONE HAS A MONTH OF VACATION every year. Not everyone can take two consecutive weeks off work whenever they want to. Sometimes obligations other than work squeeze our schedules so it's hard to even take a whole week off. But almost everyone has a weekend, and even if you can't take a whole weekend off of work, family, and housework all at once, hopefully you can take a weekend off every once in a while (if you can't, this book may turn out to provide joy only vicariously). So what can you do with 48 hours? You can climb Oregon's Mount Hood, or Mount Whitney, the tallest peak in the Lower 48. You could spend the night at a mountain hut in New Hampshire or Colorado or trek to Havasupai. You could also clean your garage and/or mow your lawn, but those things aren't covered in this book, because although they are somewhat fulfilling and—let's face it—sometimes necessary on weekends, they're not adventures, or at least not in the sense we're going for here. So set your sights on something a little bolder.

Climb Mount Hood, Oregon

LENGTH: Weekend

DESCRIPTION: If you want to see what it's like to climb a big, snowy, glaciated peak, start with Mount Hood at 11,240 feet. It's low altitude (compared to other snow climbs like Mount Rainier and higher US mountains like Mount Whitney), it has a very short technical section, and with a guide, a climb to the summit via the standard route only takes 1 day (following 1 day of learning climbing skills).

Hood, the high point of Oregon, is visible from plenty of spots in the city of Portland, above the downtown skyline. Thankfully, you don't have to climb all that elevation in one day—the parking lot at the starting point for Mount Hood climbs sits at about 5,900 feet. Summit day with a guided group covers 5,300 feet of snow climbing, the majority of which gradually ascends parallel to the Mount Hood Meadows ski resort, before tackling the final, steeper Hogsback formation through the Pearly Gates to the summit—a pitch that requires crampons and an ice axe, as well as roping up if you're in a guided group.

From the top of Mount Hood, assuming a good weather forecast, you'll see most of the famous Cascade volcanoes—Mount Rainier, Mount St. Helens, Mount Jefferson, Mount Adams, and the Three Sisters—as well as the city of Portland, far below to the west.

SEASON: Apr–June

INFO: timberlinemtguides.com

Jason Zabriskie

Climb Mount Whitney, California

LENGTH: Weekend

DESCRIPTION: The summit of the highest peak in the Lower 48 doesn't come easy. Even by its most straightforward route, the Mount Whitney Trail is 22 miles round-trip from the trailhead to the summit, and it climbs 6,100 vertical feet, which is roughly equivalent to climbing all 1,576 stairs in the Empire State Building seven times. Oh, and you have to descend all that elevation to get back to your car at the trailhead.

By the numbers, it's quite obviously worth it at that viewpoint on the crest of the clean white granite of the Sierra Nevada, the highest you can get in the United States without going to Alaska (and climbing in crampons). Otherwise, the Forest Service wouldn't have to limit the climbing permits to 195 per day between May 1 and November 1. This brings us to the second crux of the climb, aside from the physical fitness—getting a permit. Permits are distributed through a lottery system, starting February 1 of every year, and are difficult to get. To increase your chances, apply for weekday dates instead of weekends, which are the more popular.

When applying, you'll decide whether you want to tackle the whole thing in 1 day or backpack in and break the climb into 2 days. Both are tough—day hiking the trail is a very long, strenuous day, but you have a light backpack. Backpacking means you'll climb a few miles of the trail with all your camping gear for the night, then have a head start on your climbing the next morning. Either way, it's a big challenge with a big reward.

SEASON: July–Oct (best conditions in Aug–Sept)

INFO: modernhiker.com/hike/hiking-mount-whitney

Don't Let Your Suitcase Become a Ball and Chain

Jason Zabriskie

YEARS OF BACKPACKING AND CLIMBING have taught me many things, but maybe most of all, they've taught me efficiency. Just like the saying "The things you own end up owning you," packing for a trip can give you a hard-to-admit dose of reality: The things you bring can end up bringing you down.

Packing is an exercise in restraint. If you've ever packed for a few days of living with a backpack on your back, you know on the first day whether or not you've succeeded. Picking up a backpack and walking the first few steps on a trail can be a very unforgiving reality check: Man, this is heavy. Maybe I could have gone without the (a) 10-ounce flask of whiskey, or the (b) 12-ounce extra camp shoes, or the (c) 12-ounce camp pillow—or all of the above, because that's 2 pounds of extra weight!

There's another saying common to backpackers: Ounces equal pounds, and pounds equal pain. Or: All those little things add up when it comes to carrying everything you need for a week, so watch yourself when you're packing at home and not worrying about the weight on the trail.

The same is true when traveling, even if you're not walking on trails with all your gear on your back. A big suitcase can be a major pain to handle, especially if you're going to more than one destination and using public transit. A few times pulling your giant rolling suitcase out of the back of a taxi or the baggage hold on a train, or trying to hurry across a street or through a busy market, and you might find yourself wishing you had not brought those four extra pairs of shoes or that you had cut the number of shirts and pants in your luggage in half—and just brought a smaller bag.

One of the worst things you can do when you travel is try to re-create all the comforts of your home environment in a new place. If you travel enough, you're probably going to realize they don't have your favorite moisturizing lotion halfway around the world, and with any luck, they won't have your favorite restaurants from back home, either (and you'll get to try something new). You can probably live a few days without some of the "necessities" you always have at home.

If you remember that you don't need to bring your entire house with you, you'll avoid turning your suitcase into a burden during your trip. Moving efficiently, whether on the trail or between trains, can take a lot of the stress out of the adventure, and going without a few comforts can teach you a lot about yourself and open you up to new experiences in new places.

Run a Trail Ultramarathon

LENGTH: Weekend

DESCRIPTION: What's the difference between a marathon and an ultramarathon? In the purist's definition, a few feet—an ultramarathon is any distance longer than a 26.2-mile marathon. That said, you probably won't find many 26.3-mile "ultramarathons." If you poke around the Internet looking for ultras to sign up for, you'll notice that the shortest-distance ones are the 50K distance, or 31 miles. Could you run an ultramarathon? Well, it's only 4.8 miles longer than a marathon, so if you've ever run (or considered running) a marathon, you can probably handle a 50K.

A few things you should know about 50Ks: Trail running is different from road running: You're on a rougher surface with plenty of roots and rocks to watch out for as you run. If you haven't done much trail running before signing up for a trail ultramarathon, include some trail runs in your training to get used to the uneven terrain. In ultramarathons, walking is a part of the race: Many ultrarunners walk all the uphill sections of the trail and run downhills and flat sections. And last but not least, you'll need to eat. Aid stations in ultramarathons are stocked with food—actual food, often including burritos, sandwiches, chips, candy, and lots of other stuff you'd never see during a road race.

Most runners start at one of the lower-distance ultramarathon races before graduating to the 100-mile distance. There's no hard-and-fast rule that says you have to do that, but it is helpful because you'll learn lots of things in the shorter distances you can apply to a 100-mile race. Unless you have a gift for long runs, most 100-mile races will take 20 hours or more, up to 36 hours for mountain races with lots of elevation gain.

SEASON: Spring, summer, and fall

INFO: calendar.ultrarunning.com

Climb the Brigata Tridentina Via Ferrata, Italy

LENGTH: Weekend

DESCRIPTION: If you've always wanted to try outdoor rock climbing but have been intimidated by all the specialized knowledge and gear required, you'll probably love *via ferratas*—mountaineering routes equipped with ladder rungs and cables to secure yourself to where ropes might otherwise be required for safety.

Via ferratas, which means "iron ways," are most famous for their use in World War I, when troops from Italy and the Austro-Hungarian Empire fought fierce battles in the rugged northern Dolomites and needed safe methods of transporting troops and equipment around and over the steep limestone peaks. Plenty of sources say via ferratas were "invented" by the Italian army during those battles, but several routes built in Germany, Austria, and Italy were installed before the war, from 1899 to 1911.

There are more than 200 via ferrata routes in the Italian Dolomites, and the Tridentina is the most popular for good reason: It's more than 1,000 feet of vertical gain, and the climbing would be mostly 4th- and low-5th-class on the Yosemite scale. The end is a 40-foot suspension bridge from the Exner Tower to the main plateau, hanging over a 60-foot drop. The Tridentina is doable in a day but is even better as a weekend trip—climb the via ferrata one day, continue a few hundred more feet to the Rifugio Pisciadu, and stay the night, descending one of the trails the next day.

SEASON: May–Sept

INFO: holimites.com/en

flickr.com/Johannes Rainer

Rent a Car You Can Sleep In and Save $$

© iStock.com/jacoblund

IN 2007, MY FRIEND AND I WANTED TO SEE ALASKA. We didn't have much money, but we had 9 days. Boat rides, sightseeing flights, and the train all cost money —and at the time, it seemed like a lot of money.

So we rented a station wagon, which, to our delight, was just long enough for both of us to lie down inside. We could camp wherever we could find a quiet spot to park for the night, and my friend would feel more comfortable sleeping in bear country with a sturdy vehicle separating her from Alaska's wildlife (somewhat more comforting than a tent wall).

Here's one of the oldest "dirtbag" traveler tricks ever: If you can sleep in your car, you can save a ton of money. And here's a contemporary secret: It doesn't have to be some fancy camper van with a full bathroom and kitchen inside. Plenty of station wagons and SUVs have fold-down rear seats that make enough room for two average-sized people.

Yes, hotels are nice, and it's nice to shower every few days, but if you can avoid them, you don't spend as much money. Just say for a 9-day trip like we took, we had spent $100 per night on a hotel room in a different town—that's $800.

If you're sleeping in hotels, you're also beholden to a schedule—especially in places where open hotel rooms are hard to find during the busy seasons. So you make reservations in advance to make sure you have a place to sleep, and then your whole trip is structured around your hotel reservations—we have to be in Town X on the first night, Town Y the second night, Town Z the third night, and so on. There's no room for improvisation unless you want to spend more money by canceling your reservation and finding a hotel room that works with your new destination.

You don't necessarily have to have a full camping setup to sleep in a rented station wagon or SUV—a couple sleeping bags and sleeping pads are really all you need. Of course, if you have a small backpacking stove and cook every night, you can save money and have dinner in a scenic location (like the oceanfront city campground in Seward, Alaska, for example). On the other hand, if you're saving money by not sleeping in hotels every night, that's a lot more money you can spend sampling the local restaurants for breakfast and dinner.

Check your car rental rates next time you're booking a trip. Is it worth spending a couple hundred dollars more to get an SUV you can sleep in a few nights of the trip? I'd guess it might be. Just make sure you can fit most of your luggage in the front seats so you have enough room to sleep in the back.

#29

Spend a Night at a 10th Mountain Division Hut, Colorado

LENGTH: Weekend

DESCRIPTION: Ski vacations are great, but when you get there, you might realize you weren't the only one who had an idea to spend a weekend or a week skiing. Colorado's 10th Mountain Division huts provide real winter solitude and can only be accessed by skiing or snowshoeing.

Like that ski chalet you rented a few years ago, you'll have great snow-covered mountain views; but unlike that ski chalet, you won't have to wait in line with hundreds of other people when it's time to stop for lunch in the middle of your ski day. Also, unlike that ski chalet, you will have to bring everything you need in a backpack (so you'll probably be leaving behind that 12-pack of microbrews, or at least switching it out for a small bottle of whiskey). Once you're there, you'll have the place relatively to yourself—the 10th Mountain Division huts are reservation only and small capacity. If you can find 15 friends to join you for the night, you'll fill the entire hut; otherwise, you might be sharing it with one or two other parties.

The average route to a 10th Mountain Division hut is 6 miles long and gains 1,500 to 2,500 feet on the way, so you'll need backcountry skiing skills, and at least one member of your group will need to have route-finding skills and avalanche awareness. You can also hire a guide to take your group to the hut. Reservations fill up quickly and early, so start planning in summertime for a winter trip.

SEASON: Huts are available year-round, but most popular in winter.

INFO: huts.org or huts.org/Reservations/Guides.php

#30

Trek to Havasupai, Arizona

LENGTH: Weekend

DESCRIPTION: Whether you know it or not, you've probably seen a photo of Havasupai Falls somewhere: long cascades of water emptying into emerald pools in the middle of towering red and brown canyon walls.

There's a reason you don't see crowds of hundreds of people in all those photos: To reach the waterfalls, you have to walk 10 miles each way. Supai, the village near the waterfalls and the capital of the Havasupai Indian Reservation, has no road to it and can only be accessed by foot, mule, or helicopter (it's the only town in the United States where mail is still delivered by mule).

From the trailhead, hikers descend 2,300 feet over 10 miles to get to the falls, walking in full sun a lot of that time. (Of course, you'll have to reverse your route and climb all that on the way out.) After 8 miles, you'll arrive in the town of Supai, where there is a lodge, convenience store, and café. The final 2 miles to the campground access three waterfalls, and below the campground are two additional waterfalls: Mooney Falls (the tallest of the five waterfalls) and Beaver Falls (the last waterfall that requires more adventurous hiking and scrambling to access).

Campground reservations (or reservations at the lodge) are required, and day hiking to the falls from the trailhead is not allowed. Truthfully, this is not a trip you'd want to cram into a single day anyway. Two days is the minimum you'll want to spend, and 3 days is better.

SEASON: Mar–May, Sept–Oct

INFO: theofficialhavasupaitribe.com

The 3-Day Rule

flickr.com/Zach Dischner

EVER HAD THAT FEELING WHEN YOU GET AWAY for a weekend that you didn't really "get away" from anything? Like you barely got to where you were going and got your stuff unpacked before it was time to pack up and travel back home again?

It's not just you, and it's not just a feeling. You actually do need a few days just to get into a different state of mind on your vacation, something that's been theorized by guides and adventurers for a long time and that's more recently been studied by researchers. As writer Florence Williams discusses the Three-Day Effect in her book

The Nature Fix, two studies showed improved creative thinking and insight problem-solving among subjects who had been on 4- and 6-day wilderness trips.

If you've ever been on a long trip away from "the real world," you probably don't need too much scientific proof to notice there's a difference in your thinking during that trip. I've experienced it on a 28-day raft trip and multiple 7- to 10-day backpacking and kayak trips. On the first day, it seems like my brain goes back and forth between what I'm saying goodbye to (did I make my mortgage payment, did I throw out those leftovers in the fridge, did I remember to put my car keys somewhere safe so when I get back to my car I will be able to drive home, have I absolutely taken care of everything I needed to work-wise before I left?) and my new reality (where did I pack my toothbrush, did I bring enough calories for this many days out/this much mileage, is my headlamp in the top of my backpack?). On the second day, the thoughts of "home" and "work" seem to decrease to almost nothing, and on the third day, I'm able to concentrate fully on where I am and what I'm doing—not to mention I have my routine dialed in and know exactly where my toothbrush and headlamp are in my backpack.

From Day 3 onward, I'm fully engaged in the new environment. I've forgotten about my "real job," and my new job is to do all the things I need to do to make the trip a success: get up early enough to get packed and hike to the next campsite before afternoon thunderstorms roll in, take care of my feet and gear so they'll last the entire trip, pack my backpack so it's evenly weighted and everything I need is where I can find it.

After Day 3, I couldn't be less concerned with work. The questions like "What if something comes up and my coworkers don't know what to do without me there?" fade into shrugs of "They're smart; they'll figure it out." A few days later, I'm so happy with my adventure life that I wonder if I even need to go back to work at all. But then, of course, the trip ends, and I remember I get fulfillment from other things besides tramping around in nature. Back to work I go, refreshed.

If you've never experienced it, I can't recommend it enough. Give yourself a weeklong vacation—a full week, not including your travel on either end of those 7 days—and you'll see. Especially since it's scientifically proven.

#31
Overnight at a White Mountain Hut, New Hampshire

LENGTH: Weekend

DESCRIPTION: How does this sound: backpacking into the White Mountains without having to carry a tent, sleeping bag, sleeping pad, stove, pots, dinner, or breakfast? Sounds like you'll have a pretty light backpack, doesn't it? If you book a night at one of the Appalachian Mountain Club's White Mountain huts, that's exactly what will happen: You'll sleep in a bunk with a roof over your head, have a hot breakfast and dinner served to you, and enjoy great views of some of the proudest mountains in the Northeast.

Most of the White Mountain huts are a short hike from the trailhead, the longest being 4.6 miles, but they're often steep, gaining a couple thousand feet of elevation. They're all fully staffed during the summer and early fall. Two hiker shuttles run the length of the Whites during high season, and the only gear you'll need for sleeping is a lightweight sleep sack. There's also running water at the huts (although it's not heated), but as "roughing it" goes, the White Mountain huts are pretty cushy.

An overnight at a hut is a great way to spend a weekend, but if you can, a couple nights are better so you can enjoy hiking from the hut or just sitting on the porch while reading a paperback and enjoying the view. The more adventurous might consider a full traverse of the hut system over 56 miles of trail for a once-in-a-lifetime week on top of the White Mountains.

SEASON: June–mid-Oct

INFO: outdoors.org/lodging-camping/huts

FULL-DAY ADVENTURES

WHAT QUALIFIES AS A "FULL-DAY ADVENTURE"? For the purposes of this book, it's an adventure that will probably be one of the biggest, if not the best, days you've ever had in the outdoors—mountain biking Moab's 34-mile Whole Enchilada, hiking from the South Rim of the Grand Canyon to the bottom and then up to the North Rim (or vice versa), climbing a 14,000-foot peak in Colorado, or skiing Tuckerman Ravine in New Hampshire. These adventures don't require spending the night sleeping on the ground (although you're free to add that in if you'd like), but make lots of people's bucket lists. They're days that require some planning before and often a whole day (or more) to recover afterward, but will be one of (or some of) the most memorable days of your year, if you choose to take them on.

Hike a Colorado 14er

LENGTH: Full-Day

DESCRIPTION: Colorado has 54 mountains with summits higher than 14,000 feet, and despite the "thin" air at the top, they're not always that difficult to climb. In fact, many of them are Class 1 walk-ups, requiring no technical climbing skills or specialized equipment besides a sturdy pair of shoes and some extra food and clothing. Thousands of people from all over the United States travel to Colorado each summer and attempt one or more "14ers." Although not as famous as the highest 14er in the Lower 48, Mount Whitney, many of Colorado's 14ers are far more accessible—no permits are necessary, and some of the hikes are less than 10 miles round-trip.

The air up high contains less oxygen, so be prepared to slow down—often as you near the summit of a 14er, you'll find yourself stopping every 5 or 10 steps to catch your breath before climbing higher. Add to that the fact that terrain up high might feel like a never-ending Stairmaster. Even the easiest 14ers require more than 2,800 feet of elevation gain from the trailhead to the summit and hiking over and around boulders near the top.

The main precaution on a 14er: Leave early in the morning to allow yourself enough time to hike to the summit and back before afternoon thunderstorms roll in. It seems like there's a thunderstorm every summer afternoon in Colorado, and above treeline on a 14er, there's nowhere to hide. You need to be heading down from the summit by noon (if not before that), so plan on starting early and allowing yourself plenty of time to get up and down. It's not a bad idea to do a headlamp start from the trailhead before sunrise.

SEASON: Mid-June–late Sept

INFO: 14ers.com

Sleeping in a Tent Is Not That Comfortable (But If You Can Handle It for a Couple Nights, It Will Change Your Life)

© iStock.com/Justin Buchli

WHEN I WAS ON THE DENALI NATIONAL PARK BUS TOUR in Alaska several years ago, I met a retired firefighter from Lincoln, Nebraska, named Fred. Fred had driven all the way from Nebraska to Alaska, along the ALCAN, all by himself.

Fred said he camped out every other night on his trip and stayed in a hotel on the other nights. That way, he could have a shower and a bed every second night. I thought this was genius, not fully committing to either of the two opposing travel styles: those who must stay in a bed every night and those who must camp every night. Fred was cutting his trip costs probably in half just by carrying a sleeping bag and a tent in his car and sleeping under the stars half the time.

Camping is not the most comfortable thing in the world—and probably no one who does it would tell you they do it because it's comfortable. It's cold, or sometimes hot, and if you have to go to the bathroom in the middle of the night, you have to unzip a sleeping bag and get yourself up off the ground. There's no running water, it's harder to wash dishes, you usually cook on only one or two burners, and things are generally just less convenient.

But, as Fred illustrated, it can make the world your oyster. It can make unaffordable trips suddenly affordable, it can make the inflexible schedules dictated by hotel reservations flexible, and if you do it, I guarantee you'll see way more sunsets and sunrises.

Camping, to me, isn't a lifestyle. It's a tactic. I've spent months on the road, living out of my car, something I never would have been able to do if I told myself I absolutely had to stay in an Embassy Suites every night of my vacation. They don't build many affordable hotels on California and Oregon oceanfronts, or in thick stands of Montana and Washington old-growth trees, or in the Utah and Arizona deserts. But there are plenty of campsites in those places, and I've enjoyed some pretty fantastic views while brushing my teeth standing next to my car or my tent instead of in some sterile hotel room bathroom.

Camping doesn't have to be your favorite thing in the world to turn a $3,000 road trip vacation into a $500 road trip vacation. It's a means to see more of the world with the money you have, and if you do it, you'll probably see way more of the world because you won't have hotel walls blocking your view. It's not always sunny, warm, and cushy, but if you do it enough times, it actually might turn out to be your favorite thing in the world.

#33

Ski Tuckerman Ravine, New Hampshire (in Spring)

LENGTH: Full-Day

DESCRIPTION: Skiing Tuckerman Ravine on Mount Washington's south-eastern face is a tradition that's been going on since the 1930s, when the Civilian Conservation Corps cut a ski trail from Pinkham Notch to the base of the ravine and built a warming hut, making access easier and paving the way for ski races. It's one of the most famous rites of passage for East Coast skiers, filling the parking on the sides of the road at the trailhead and the 3-mile trail itself. Some people show up to ski the famous bowl, and some just show up to watch.

It's not full-on backcountry skiing—the season for most skiers is in late April and early May, after the snowpack has consolidated—but it's not beginner skiing either. The easiest line of the 10 lines is 35–45 degrees, and the only way to get to the top is to bootpack all the way. Oh, and the hike to get to the base of the bowl takes most people about 3 hours. If you fall and get injured, there's no ski patrol to come to your aid. That said, serious accidents are fairly rare, and if you're a confident black-diamond skier, Tucks is a fun adventure and unique to East Coast skiing in that it's a long, run-out ski path with no trees in the way.

Wear a helmet, practice your steep turns during ski season before you go, and be ready for some quad-burning hiking before your run down.

SEASON: Late Apr–early May (dependent on snowpack)

INFO: cathedralmountainguides.com

Kit Noble

34

Ride the Whole Enchilada, Moab, Utah

LENGTH: Full-Day

DESCRIPTION: If you love long mountain bike rides with expansive desert vistas, the Whole Enchilada is for you. If you prefer your long mountain bike rides to have a 5½-to-1 downhill-to-uphill ratio, the Whole Enchilada is really for you: It's 34 miles of riding, lots of technical descending, and a fair amount of fire road. You'll start in the mountains at 10,500 feet and climb to 11,150 feet before descending almost 8,000 feet into the desert over the course of the day. Total uphill pedaling: 1,400 feet.

By most mountain biking standards, the Whole Enchilada is a huge day in the saddle. Expert mountain bikers love it, intermediate bikers will find it to be a good challenge, and everyone who's ever pedaled a mountain bike in Moab will wonder about it until they've done it at least once.

The best way to experience the ride is to take a shuttle van to the top (you're more than welcome to ride the 7,900 feet of ascent from town up to the start, but it's rare) for $30 per person. Pack enough water, food, and sunscreen for a big day. Also, do yourself a favor by riding a couple Moab-area trails before taking this one on, so you can get used to the terrain first. Riding it on a hardtail is possible (technically everything is), but most riders will want a full-suspension bike. If you don't own one, plenty of shops in Moab will let you demo one for the day.

SEASON: May–Oct (September and October have the best temperatures.)

INFO: wholeenchiladashuttles.com

flickr.com/Stanislav Sedov

The Second Most Famous Hike Somewhere Can Be Great (and Without Crowds)

COLORADO'S 14,060-FOOT MOUNT BIERSTADT is one of the most popular "14er" hikes in the state—it's a 1½-hour drive from the urban center of Denver, it's a short hike at 7 miles round-trip, and it's the easiest trail to the top of all the 58 14,000-foot peaks in the state. Even on weekday mornings, if you hike it, you'll be accompanied by 100 to 300 people—and weekends are even more popular.

Just across the street—or, more accurately, across Guanella Pass Road—there's another mountain: Square Top Mountain. It's a 6.5-mile hike to a 13,794-foot summit, has great views of the Colorado Rockies from the top, and is relatively ignored compared to its neighbor across the way. Why? Because people just want to climb a 14er in Colorado, and Square Top is 206 feet shy of that title.

Now, this doesn't bother me a bit—I'll take the solitude whenever I can get it, and I think everyone should take the opportunity to check "climbing a 14er" off their list when they can. But it illustrates something I've noticed about the outdoors: Right next to the really popular (and sometimes even crowded) thing, there's a pretty good alternative.

This is especially true in national parks: Hundreds of people do the 3-mile round-trip hike to Delicate Arch in Arches National Park, and it feels crowded because you're all headed to the same viewpoint at the end: the one right in front of Delicate Arch. But a few miles up the road, you can do a longer hike on the Devils Garden Loop, see several striking and varied arches, and see way fewer people at each one. Same thing with Angels Landing (crowded) and Observation Point (not nearly as crowded) in Zion National Park or Chasm Lake (popular) and Black Lake (almost no one there) in Rocky Mountain National Park.

Obviously, the popular places are popular for good reason—they're beautiful, great experiences, and often attainable for most people. But as the saying goes, "Nothing draws a crowd like a crowd." Lots of people go to those popular, big-name spots just because they're well known and it's easy to find information about them online or through word of mouth. If you do a little more research, you might find a lot more solitude.

One thing you can do when visiting a national park is ask a ranger or other employee at an information center, "What's the most popular hike in the park?" When they answer, you can say, "Okay, so we should avoid that. Where do you go when you're not working?" You'll get an answer that will probably lead you to a place that's just as great as "the most popular hike in the park" but with way fewer people.

35

Hike the Zion Narrows, Utah

LENGTH: Full-Day

DESCRIPTION: As you wind up Zion Canyon in one of the Zion National Park shuttle buses, the walls get closer and closer together until you're craning your neck and smooshing your face against the window of the bus trying to see the tops of the formations thousands of feet above the road along the canyon floor. By the time the bus reaches the back of the canyon, you might have noticed some passengers wearing strange-looking water shoes and carrying hiking sticks or trekking poles. They're going to do a one-of-a-kind hike called "the Narrows."

The Narrows are where the walls of Zion Canyon rise straight up from the banks of the Virgin River, with towering sandstone walls only a few dozen feet apart. The hike begins where the concrete riverwalk trail ends, and you step right into the river and walk upstream. It's a unique hike with unique gear needs, and you should definitely consider trekking poles or a hiking stick, as well as water shoes. You don't have to buy specific water shoes just for this hike—rent them at outfitters in nearby Springdale, or just wear a pair of nonwaterproof hiking shoes or trail-running shoes (waterproof shoes will fill up with water and weigh a ton). Consider neoprene socks to keep your feet warm. Take a drybag for clothes, food, and electronics that you don't want to get wet.

The great thing about the Narrows is that you can have a great experience no matter how far you go. Most people suggest taking 6 to 8 hours to get to the best spots on the hike, but even a few minutes upriver and back will deliver some great views.

SEASON: Summer–fall

INFO: nps.gov/zion

36

Hike Mount Si, Washington

LENGTH: Full-Day

DESCRIPTION: Mount Si is one of the most popular hikes in the Northwest, thanks to the views from the top (you can see Mount Rainier on a clear day), its length (8 miles round-trip), and its proximity to Seattle (45 minutes from downtown with no traffic). But it also stymies plenty of hikers, thanks to its steepness—the trail gains 3,150 feet from trailhead to summit and is a walk in the park for no one.

But that makes it a proud day hike. More than 100,000 people start up the trail each year, grinding up the endless switchbacks through old-growth forest to the top of the trail. The views from the top of the hike peek into the Cascades, the Olympics all the way on the other side of Seattle, and to Mount Rainier to the south. The true summit of the Haystack, the rocky outcrop at the top of Mount Si, can be reached with a few hundred feet of scrambling. **CAUTION:** Be warned; it's exposed and serious, and a fall could very likely be fatal.

Mount Si is used as a training hike for many who have their sights set on Mount Rainier and a great intro to the terrain of the peaks of the Pacific Northwest and the Cascades, the sea of craggy, glaciated peaks to the north. Even if you don't ever climb anything else in the Northwest, Mount Si is a proud hike.

SEASON: Year-round, although winter hikes might require trail crampons

INFO: wta.org/go-hiking/hikes/mount-si

What to Rent and What to Buy

Mike Bezemek

YOU'RE PLANNING YOUR DREAM ADVENTURE TRIP, and like a lot of things, it requires a lot of specialized gear, which can get expensive. What can you do? Here's one idea: Don't buy every single piece of gear.

For example, to climb Mount Hood with a guide, you need mountaineering boots ($300), crampons ($130), an ice axe ($80), a climbing helmet ($60), and a climbing harness ($50)—not to mention the clothing you may or may not already own. That's

$620 in specialized gear you're buying without knowing if you'll even like mountaineering enough to do another climb.

Here's how you save some money: One guide service will rent you crampons, mountaineering boots, and an ice axe for $66 for the entire climb and will let you borrow a harness and helmet for free. Congratulations, you just saved yourself $554 on the cost of your climb (almost enough to pay for a friend to join you!).

In 2015, my girlfriend and I planned a bike tour in northern Norway. We could have shipped our own bikes there for $100 apiece each way, plus purchased racks and panniers for the bikes to carry all our gear ($420 per person), a total of $620 per person. But a bike shop in Tromso rents fully equipped touring bikes for $25/day. For our 10-day trip, that would cost us $250 each, saving $370 each. Also, we wouldn't have to worry about our bikes getting damaged flying to and from Norway. It was a no-brainer for us—we rented the bikes, rode them for 10 days, and had a blast.

You may not want to rent everything—mountaineering boots, for example, can be a personal choice. If you have issues with shoes fitting correctly or find yourself getting blisters, you might want to buy your own mountaineering boots. You can always use them as hiking boots (they're a little bit of overkill for that, but they work just fine and allow you to get more out them than just a onetime investment). Rental skis and boots are another personal choice—if you're only skiing a few days every year, it makes sense to rent skis and boots. If you have bad luck with rental boots fitting you, you might want to buy your own boots and just rent skis. If you don't like to travel with skis (it's not that much fun hauling your ski bag around an airport), you can always use your own boots and rent skis when you get to the resort.

There's no magic equation for renting vs. buying—a lot of it comes down to personal choice and what you want to keep in your garage or house after your trip is over. Buying all the gear for a onetime thing can be a costly way to collect souvenirs, and a kayak, for example, takes up a lot more room than a pair of crampons. Just do a little research and understand your options, then figure out what works best for your needs on that specific trip.

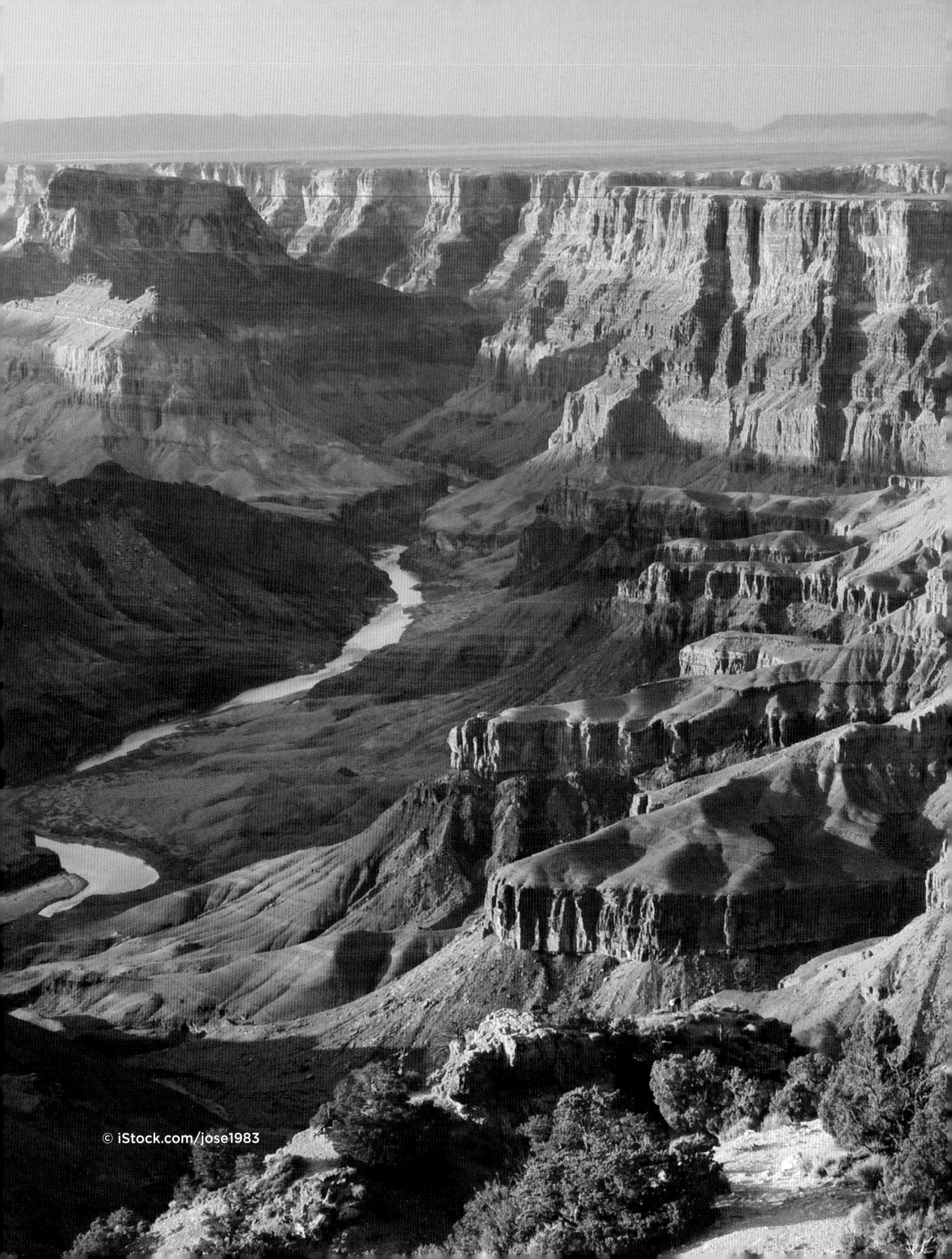

Hike from Rim to Rim in the Grand Canyon, Arizona

LENGTH: Full-Day

DESCRIPTION: Imagine hiking to the summit of a mountain, covering almost a vertical mile of elevation gain, and then going back down again over the course of a long day of 23 miles of moving. Okay, now imagine doing it in reverse—down first and summit second. That's what hiking from one rim of the Grand Canyon to another is like, except, of course, you're walking all the way across one of America's most famous national parks, and you have to get a ride back to your car when you're done.

A rim-to-rim hike of the Grand Canyon (or vice versa) is so highly coveted it's very difficult to get a backpacking permit for a 3- or 4-day leisurely experience. Instead, many opt to hike from one rim to another in one day, a challenge but doable by any fit weekend warrior who can move at a decent clip. The mileage for the hike is the same in both directions, but since the North Rim is 1,400 feet higher in elevation than the South Rim, hiking south to north is a bit more strenuous than north to south.

Either way is a fantastic trek through millions of years of geology visible in the distinct layers of canyon rock. Hikers should take plenty of food and water (you'll be able to refill bottles at the bottom), a headlamp, and appropriate layers of clothing for temperature changes throughout the day and through different elevations. A 4-hour van shuttle takes hikers between the rims during high season, but plan for lodging at the rim where your hike ends—the shuttle leaves in the morning not in the evening. Alternately, plan for a friend to drive your car around to pick you up at the end of your trek.

SEASON: Late Sept–mid-Oct

INFO: nps.gov/grca, trans-canyonshuttle.com

#38

Learn to Ice Climb, New Hampshire

LENGTH: Full-Day

DESCRIPTION: If you can wrap your head around rock climbing without thinking, "That's crazy!" then surely climbing up a frozen waterfall with ice picks in your hands and spikes on your feet doesn't strike you as that far-fetched.

  A couple tips: The things in your hands are actually called *ice tools*, and the spikes on your feet are actually called *crampons*. Ice climbing is cold, but if you've ever gotten cold while ice-skating or skiing and decided you were still having fun despite the temperatures, you'll probably be fine ice climbing. Also, you don't need to be a superhero who can do 200 pull-ups in a row to be able to climb ice. Most people will tell you that you don't even need to be able to do one pull-up (but it might help a little bit).

  New Hampshire, with its cold winter temps and wetter mountain climate, has some of the best ice climbing in North America, from steep frozen waterfalls to long ice and snow gullies in the White Mountains. Like rock climbing, ice climbing requires special gear and training (including ropes), but a guide can teach you the basic skills in a day and take you up a classic climb the next day (depending on your comfort level on the ice and with the equipment). It's cold and maybe a little difficult to explain to your coworkers on Monday morning, but it's also one of the most exhilarating experiences you can have outdoors.

SEASON: Dec–Mar

INFO: cathedralmountainguides.com/new-hampshire-ice-climbing

The Joys of Camping
on a Weeknight

© iStock.com/IanVorster

EVERY YEAR ON MEMORIAL DAY WEEKEND and Labor Day weekend, I watch a mass migration from my hometown of Denver as thousands of cars clog the interstates and highways to head out of town and go camping. If you didn't know better, you might think these two weekends were the only possible times of the year to go camping in Colorado.

Here's a secret: They're not. You can camp on any weekend, and if you're strategic about it, you can even camp on a weeknight. That's right. Here's one more secret:

Almost no one goes camping on weeknights, so all those campgrounds and campsites near where you live and that fill every Friday and Saturday night during the summer are empty and quiet the other 5 nights a week.

Yes, it's not a 3-day weekend. Yes, if you camp on a weeknight, you might have to sacrifice your eggs-and-bacon camp breakfast in order to make it into the office on time the next morning. But time in nature is time in nature, however you get it. If you normally like to eat three slices of pizza at a time and someone instead offered you (a) one slice of pizza or (b) no pizza at all, which would you choose? I'd choose option a every time.

So, how can you get a weeknight outside? Find a state park or county park near your town, pack the car the night before, and leave work an hour early just like you would if your kids had a baseball game or a dentist appointment. Get out of town, set up your tent, cook dinner, and enjoy escaping your routine for a night. Wake up early the next morning, eat a quick breakfast, and head home to shower before work—or better yet, sleep in a little bit and see if you can get away without showering before heading into the office. This usually works best on Casual Fridays.

Small doses of nature are good for you, and you might discover that it's a lot less hectic to do a few nights of camping on summer weeknights instead of joining the hordes leaving town for those two long weekends. When I used to work in an office, I would set a goal of sleeping outside for 30 nights every year. With a couple weeks' vacation, as many weekends as possible during the spring, summer, and fall, and a few weeknights during the summer, I always reached my goal.

Not every one of those weeknights camping was fantastic, but I'll tell you what: They were way better than staying home and feeling the pressure to do laundry, answer e-mails, do small housework jobs, or run errands. And when you're sitting by a campfire on a Thursday night with hardly a neighbor around at a campground that will be full the next night, you really feel like you're getting away with something. Even if you're only 12 or 13 miles from your house.

#39

Take the Denali National Park Bus Tour, Alaska

LENGTH: Full-Day

DESCRIPTION: How would you like to have the chance to spend 11 hours on a school bus? Not interested? How about if the bus were driving into Denali National Park on the only road into the park, where cars aren't allowed?

Short of skiing into the park by yourself, the Denali National Park shuttle bus is the easiest way to see the tundra, rivers, and huge mountains that make the park famous. The shuttle bus drives the dirt Denali Park Road from near the park entrance 85 miles into the park, stopping at viewpoints along the way and finally for lunch at Wonder Lake, where, if you're lucky, you'll get a view of the park's 20,320-foot-high namesake peak. Then you'll head back. The bus ride is not narrated, but if you're lucky, you'll see some of the park's megafauna—moose, caribou, grizzly bears, and even wolves. All this for less than $50 per person.

Narrated bus tours of the park are available, including going even farther down the park road to the old gold mining town of Kantishna, for around $200 per person.

SEASON: June–mid-Sept

INFO: reservedenali.com

flickr.com/Dankarl

Climb Katahdin, Maine

LENGTH: Full-Day

DESCRIPTION: The highest point in the state of Maine, the summit of Katahdin, is about 10 feet lower than the city of Denver, but its reputation is more than a mile high. It's most famous as the northern terminus of the 2,190-mile Appalachian Trail, a majestic end point for trekkers who started their journey 6 months prior in Georgia.

The name *Katahdin* doesn't refer to a single summit but to a massif with seven subpeaks: Baxter Peak, the actual summit (5,270 feet); South Peak (5,260 feet); Pamola Peak (4,919 feet); Chimney Peak (4,900 feet); Hamlin Peak (4,756 feet); South Howe Peak (4,740 feet); and North Howe Peak (4,700 feet). The treeline is much lower at Katahdin's high altitude (between 3,500 and 3,800 feet), meaning the upper 1,500 feet of the mountain is exposed glacially carved granite, and there are views in every direction.

The most famous ridge on Katahdin is the Knife Edge, a 1,500-foot section of 3-foot-wide ridge with a 1,000-plus-foot drop on either side. It's worth watching your step up there. On rare occasions, hikers have slipped off during rainy or snowy weather, and on even rarer occasions, hikers have been blown off the ridge. However, most make it safely through the traverse to the summit. There are many routes to the summit, and the Knife Edge is only one of them. The most popular trail to the top is the 5.2-mile Hunt Trail, almost half of which is above treeline.

SEASON: Mid-May–mid-Oct

INFO: baxterstatepark.org

Chris Shane

You Don't Have to Leave the Country to Have an Adventure

Chris Shane

WHEN I WAS FIRST GETTING INTO THE OUTDOORS, a friend and I decided to climb Borah Peak in Idaho, the tallest mountain in the state. Halfway up the start of the scrambling to the summit, we came upon a couple also headed to the top. While chatting, we discovered that they were on a trip out west from Pennsylvania to climb a bunch of state highpoints—Borah Peak in Idaho, Wheeler Peak in New Mexico, and a few others. The man said something that's always stuck with me: "Americans do all this traveling all over the world, and they've never seen this."

It was a pretty good place for him to say something like that, looking over the mountains rising high above the plains of eastern Idaho, and I think he had a valid point: There's plenty to keep us busy, and in awe, right in our own backyards, if we just look for it.

Now, I would never discourage anyone from traveling internationally, for the many rewards it offers (not the least of which is seeing another culture's priorities). But sometimes those across-the-ocean trips are tough for varying reasons—too much time off work, too much money this year, not affordable for a family with kids. And in those cases, I don't think we should shrug our shoulders and say, "Well, we can't afford to go to India this year, so we might as well give up on having any fun."

We have mountains in our own country—on both coasts, as you know. We have access to thousands of miles of ocean coastline, tons of lakes and rivers, and thousands of miles of trails. Yes, not all of our trails lead to the summit of something like Mount Fuji, and not every surf spot is as good as the North Shore of Waikiki. But if you just get out there, whether it's a national park two or three states away or a county park 20 minutes away, I think you'll find there are plenty of things that are more rewarding than another weekend of binge-watching Netflix shows (not that that's not rewarding in its own way, but let's be honest, you can binge-watch Netflix shows anytime).

I'm willing to bet that if you take a look at a map of where you live, you can find at least a handful of things you haven't done—trails you haven't hiked, places you haven't camped, creeks or rivers you haven't floated or fished, maybe even miles of paved bike paths you haven't pedaled (and maybe at the end of those bike paths, bakeries you've never been to). You don't have to leave the country to have an adventure. You probably don't even have to leave your state. And, depending on where you live and your perspective, you may not even have to leave your county.

Ride the Monarch Crest Trail, Colorado

LENGTH: Full-Day

DESCRIPTION: If you were to announce to a room full of veteran mountain bikers that you thought the Monarch Crest Trail was the best ride you'd ever done, you wouldn't hear a lot of arguing. The 34-mile trail in Colorado's high country has made it on dozens of Top 10 lists throughout the years, and rightly so: single-track winding in and out of wide-open, high-altitude mountain views, enough climbing to feel like you've earned the views, and 6,000 feet of descending.

The ride begins on Monarch Pass, elevation 11,312 feet, and climbs to just under 12,000 feet before starting its epic descent. It's not "all downhill from there," however. There are plenty of small climbs throughout the ride, and most riders who finish it say it feels like a lot more uphill riding than the approximately 2,000 feet it's usually billed as having.

Show up in shape. If you haven't been on a few 5- or 6-hour mountain bike rides with some substantial ascent and descent before signing up for a Monarch Pass ride, you'll probably get a little beaten up by that sort of ride at high altitude. Know the route and arrange your own car shuttle to the beginning and end, or go on a group ride with a local bike shop, with demo bike provided in the cost.

SEASON: Mid-July–late Sept

INFO: absolutebikesadventures.com/guided-rides/monarch-crest-trail

flickr.com/Zach Dischner

Climb Mount Fuji, Japan

LENGTH: Full-Day

DESCRIPTION: Understand one thing if you decide to climb Mount Fuji: You're not doing it for the solitude. It's more of a cultural experience on a mountain. It's far from a wilderness experience, with vendors selling food and drinks, sleeping huts and hostels on the way up, and more than 300,000 people attempting to make it to the summit every year— mostly during the official climbing season from early July to early September.

But, unlike shopping the day after Thanksgiving, braving the crowds on Mount Fuji is actually worth it, especially if you get to the top in time to see sunrise. And don't be lulled into complacency by the number of hikers. It's still a mountain, with mountain weather, high altitude, and changing conditions. It's 12,389 feet tall, and if you climb the most common route, the Yoshida route, you'll ascend almost 5,000 feet by the time you get to the summit.

To get to the top by sunrise, you'll climb by headlamp, somewhere in the endless stream of other climbers' headlamps and flashlights. If you make it in time and have clear weather, you might see Mount Fuji's shadow stretching 15 miles long down on the valley floor and the lights of nearby Tokyo.

SEASON: Early July–early Sept

INFO: fujisan-climb.jp/en

© iStock.com/Sean Pavone

Why You Should Have Both the AAA Card and the AAC Card

© iStock.com/nautiluz56

FACT: IF YOUR CAR BREAKS DOWN ON THE SIDE OF A HIGHWAY in the desert, miles from nowhere, you don't have to have a AAA card to get your car towed to the nearest town to get fixed. But depending on your membership level and the distance to said nearest town, if you do have a AAA card, you could get your car towed for free, which is pretty nice.

My girlfriend and I travel a lot, sometimes together, sometimes separately, and our total AAA couples' membership costs less than $80 a year. We use our cards separately for hotel discounts, Amtrak ticket discounts, and thankfully, we rarely have to use it for roadside assistance, towing, or jump-starts (but those are also benefits).

I don't work for AAA—I just like to be prepared and not spend unnecessary money, so I recommend the AAA card to people who travel a lot. If you spend 10 nights a year in a hotel and save $10 on each hotel room, the card has paid for itself.

Most people have heard of AAA, but not everyone's heard of the AAC—the American Alpine Club. Even if you're not a mountain climber, you should have an AAC membership (also less than $80/year). Why? For one thing, you can take advantage of the AAC's rescue insurance if you ever hurt yourself in the mountains and need a rescue —that includes spraining your ankle 3 miles from the trailhead on a day hike.

The AAC card will also get you deals on outdoor gear, discounts on lodging in mountain huts all over the world, and discounts on accommodations at climbers' hostels and campgrounds in places like Grand Teton National Park. And perhaps my favorite membership benefit: the American Alpine Club library, which will lend you any of its hundreds of international hiking and climbing guidebooks by mail. So if you're going to Italy to hike the Alta Via 1 in the Dolomites, you can get a guidebook and discounts on every mountain hut you stay in over the course of your trip—and if you happen to need a helicopter rescue, you're covered for that, too.

Both cards are very low-cost insurance policies in their own ways and I think a worthy—but minimal—investment for anyone who wants to have adventures big or small and live to tell about them.

HALF-DAY ADVENTURES

MANY OF THE HALF-DAY ADVENTURES ON OUR LIST TAKE ONLY A FEW HOURS but leave a lasting impression: from BASE jumping off a bridge, to climbing above the breath-taking exposure of Angels Landing in Zion National Park, to rafting the nearly nonstop whitewater of the Middle Ocoee River or riding the train through the tunnel in the Eiger. The half-day trips that made the cut are a diverse set of outings that will blow your hair back, but all for completely different reasons. And then, of course, you'll still have the rest of your day to kick back, have a burger and/or a beer, and think about what a great day it was.

43

Hike Angels Landing, Utah

LENGTH: Half-Day

DESCRIPTION: Probably no trail in the United States offers more adventure per mile than Angels Landing, an exposed traverse 1,200 feet above the floor of Zion Canyon, with chains for handholds. It's not for the faint of heart, but those who venture out to the end of the "trail" are rewarded with a one-of-a-kind view of the canyon from a sandstone pedestal towering over the Virgin River.

The entire hike to the top of Angels Landing is only 2.4 miles one way, but the approach is a relentless climb up a path, gaining 1,500 feet in elevation, almost all of it before the chained section that leads to the viewpoint at the end. If you're not sure about heights, don't worry: You'll have a chance to change your mind before starting the exposed section and a good place to rest and wait if some of your party chooses to continue. It is easy to turn around in the first part of the chains section if you start and decide it's not for you.

Angels Landing is one of the most popular hikes in Zion National Park, so go early to avoid traffic on the chains. Only one person at a time can cross each chained section safely. The route is open year-round but can be snow and ice covered in winter and very warm in the summer. Spring and fall will provide the best temperatures and less company on the route.

SEASON: Mar–Nov

INFO: nps.gov/zion

© iStock.com/gelyngfjell

44

Tandem BASE Jump from the Perrine Bridge, Idaho

LENGTH: Half-Day

DESCRIPTION: If you want to do a tandem skydive, where you jump out of a plane while attached to an experienced, qualified instructor who will pull the rip cord and ensure you have a safe landing thousands of feet below, you probably don't have to drive too far in the contiguous United States. If you want to do a tandem BASE jump, there's only one place in the United States to do it: Twin Falls, Idaho.

A tandem BASE jump is different from skydiving in a number of ways: You're not jumping out of a plane; you're jumping off a structure or cliff (BASE stands for Building, Antenna, Span, Earth). *Span* means bridge in many cases, and that's the only place in America where you can do a tandem BASE jump: the 486-foot-high Perrine Bridge over the Snake River, just north of Twin Falls.

Like skydiving, you'll be strapped to an experienced, qualified instructor whose primary mission is to keep both of you alive (which is good for business), and you'll jump into a free fall. Unlike skydiving, you won't have airplane noise; it'll be a peaceful if adrenaline-charged moment. The free fall will be a lot shorter because, instead of being thousands of feet in the air in a plane, you'll be 486 feet above the Snake River, which, when you're standing looking down at it, seems plenty high. After the chute opens, you'll float down to river level and either hike out of the canyon or get picked up by a boat.

SEASON: Year-round, weather permitting

INFO: tandembase.com

flickr.com/Ben Keith

Great Places Are Crowded But Only in a Few Spots

© iStock.com/YURY TARANIK

MAYBE YOU'VE HEARD OF UTAH'S FAMOUS DELICATE ARCH or even shared the view of it with 200 other people at sunset in high season. Maybe you've heard of the Grand Canyon or been on the South Rim when another tour bus unloads and you suddenly find yourself looking into the chasm with hundreds of new friends from all over the world. It might be easy to think to yourself, "This place is so crowded," and then, "Let's get out of here."

But here's a not-very-well-kept secret: Lots of these places are only crowded in certain areas, and most of those areas are the ones that are the easiest to get to. Think about it: If you were planning your dream vacation, wouldn't you want to have all the best stuff and prefer it to come with minimal to no effort? Well, so would everyone else, so we gravitate to those places that are easy: the roadside viewpoints where we can take photos without having to walk miles upon miles (actually a few hundred feet or less would be great, thanks). If we're hiking, especially with small children or family members who aren't in condition to do a 10-mile hike, we'll flock to waterfalls or rock formations less than a mile from the parking lot or popular short hikes. It's human nature.

So if you want to escape the crowds, it's pretty simple: Pick objectives far away from parking lots. If there's cool stuff close to the parking lot, there's cool stuff far from the parking lot, too. It just might not be as famous because fewer people have been there. If you're willing to put on a pair of hiking shoes, pack a lunch, and walk a few miles into the backcountry for the day, you'll see fewer people the farther you go. Even better, if you're willing to pack a backpack with a couple days' worth of food and hike even farther from the road, you might feel as though you have the whole place to yourselves, and you might not see anyone at all.

Like anything else worth having, solitude is something you have to put in a little extra effort to get sometimes—especially in beautiful places. It's not that those popular—or crowded—places aren't great. Everyone should take the time to see the Grand Canyon from the South Rim and Delicate Arch, even if you have to share it with a couple hundred other people. But after that, find something far away from those popular places, and go have your own experience, without the crowds.

#45

Hike to Ski Highland Bowl, Aspen Highlands Ski Resort, Colorado

LENGTH: Half-Day

DESCRIPTION: If you want to ski backcountry terrain from the top of a 12,000-foot peak but don't have the avalanche training and equipment, Aspen Highlands' Highland Bowl will deliver that experience for a small cardiovascular price: an 800-vertical-foot hike to the top of Highland Peak before you can ski down double-black-diamond terrain.

Highland Bowl's relatively safe snowpack isn't some lucky weather or terrain miracle. The snow in Highland Bowl is packed by a force of local volunteers who plod down the bowl in ski boots for 15 eight-hour days each winter in order to earn a ski pass. Their sweat and toil make your magical experience possible.

You'll take a ski lift to the top of lift-served terrain, put your boots in walk mode, and start hiking the 782 feet to the 12,392-foot summit. Locals and fit skiers can hike it in 30 minutes or less, but most folks take closer to an hour to get to the top. From the summit, you'll have your choice of steep classic lines to descend. But first, enjoy the view of snowy peaks in every direction.

SEASON: Christmas–Mar

INFO: aspensnowmass.com

Jordan Curet

46

Raft the Middle Ocoee River, Tennessee

LENGTH: Half-Day

DESCRIPTION: If you've never been whitewater rafting, you might be surprised to find out that it's not one continuous period of bouncing through rapids with your heart in your throat. There are actually flat stretches where you can catch your breath and adjust your helmet. That's true for most whitewater raft trips, anyway, but quite a bit less so on Tennessee's Middle Ocoee River, which is advertised as "90 percent whitewater" and "5 miles of almost continuous Class 3 and 4 rapids."

Factually, yes, there are 20 Class 3 and Class 4 rapids in a 5-mile stretch, so no one's really exaggerating. Guided trips on the Middle Ocoee are beginner-friendly and family-friendly affairs (for kids over 12 years old): a 1½- to 2-hour trip on the river (3½ hours total including shuttles to and from), with an experienced guide to direct your boat and ensure safety.

The Middle Ocoee is America's most popular raft trip, with more than 200,000 paddlers experiencing it each year, but it's not really open for business every day. The river is controlled by dam release, meaning the dam upriver from the whitewater sections releases water on specific days, only on weekends during some of the spring and fall months, and almost every day during the summer. Rafting companies schedule their trips around those big waves of whitewater coming out of the dam.

SEASON: Mar–Oct

INFO: ocoeerafting.com

Mike Bezemek

Commit to Plans
Early and Often

© iStock.com/AlizadaStudios

EVER WONDER HOW "CERTAIN PEOPLE" MANAGE to do all sorts of cool stuff every year? Do you find yourself commenting, online or just to yourself, "How do they have time for all that?" Here's a simple math concept: No one has more time than anyone else. We just choose to use it differently.

Obviously, there are some exceptions here; for example, if you're doing your medical residency, you probably don't have many hours outside of work to devote to, say, making pottery or learning to play the didgeridoo. But for the most part, we're all working

40–50 hours a week, have 2 days off every week, and have a couple weeks of vacation time every year. Some people use all that time to climb mountains and travel, some people use it to spend time with their kids, and some people use it to watch television. How you spend your leisure time is up to you, and if you need to use all of it to "relax," this probably isn't the book for you.

The reason those "certain people" do all that cool stuff is they commit. They make plans, stick with them, and see them through. They don't sit around in a bar talking about "someday I'd really like to see the Matterhorn" and then procrastinate it. They're at home, searching for plane tickets to Zurich, trains to Zermatt, hotels, and then checking their bank account balance and work schedule to see when they can make it happen. If they want to go mountain biking with a friend on Saturday, they nail down a time to meet on Saturday morning: 8 a.m. at the trailhead. They don't half-ass a plan with their friend and say, "Give me a call when you wake up on Saturday, and we'll play it by ear." Those half-ass plans are usually better at accomplishing hangover brunch than they are at setting up a mountain bike ride with a friend.

Here's one thing that's always worked for me: Take care of the most expensive part of the trip first. This is usually the plane tickets. Do your research of where you're going, buy the tickets a few months in advance, and then sort out the rest of the plan later. You've bought your $600–800 plane ticket, which also happens to be a pain to reschedule—most airline change fees are more than $200, which is one-fourth to one-third the price of your ticket. See, it's pretty hard to change it now, isn't it? This is commitment.

Don't make plans with people who flake on plans. Find someone who's just as excited as you are to go backpacking in the Grand Canyon, and pick a date that works for both of you. Four months in advance, get the permit, buy the flights to Las Vegas, and reserve the rental car to drive to the South Rim. Boom. Now you have 4 months of paychecks with which to pay for those costs, and 4 months to sit around and look at maps and photos of the Grand Canyon in anticipation of your trip. And let me tell you, anticipation is way more gratifying than sitting around waffling about whether or not you should go, or have time for the trip, or have enough money, or whatever. You have to go now. That question is answered. You've committed, and now nobody's barbecue, golf outing, or home improvement project can get in the way of that weekend because you've marked it off on your calendar as "Grand Canyon Trip," and you won't even be in town to do anything else. You'll be too busy enjoying the views—because you made a plan and stuck with it.

47

Climb the Third Flatiron, Colorado

LENGTH: Half-Day

DESCRIPTION: Climber and Patagonia founder Yvon Chouinard legendarily called the Third Flatiron "the best beginner rock climb in the universe," and if you do it once, it's easy to see why. It's easily accessible—only a half-hour hike from the parking lot at Chautauqua Park in Boulder, Colorado. It doesn't require a high level of climbing experience. As you climb, you'll almost always have your hands wrapping around two good handholds, and the angle isn't steep. The climb is 800 feet long, leading to a summit about the size of a van, which feels like an eagle's nest.

Climbing guides will require some multipitch rock climbing experience before taking you up the Third Flatiron (to make sure you know to belay and are comfortable on the three rappels off the back of the formation). If you don't have multipitch experience, they'll lead you through a 2-hour intro course the evening before your climb.

The next day, it's on to the grippy sandstone for the time of your life. You'll spend hours climbing 8 to 10 pitches to the summit and only have birds and other climbers for company as you enjoy the views of Boulder far below.

SEASON: Aug–Jan

INFO: coloradomountainschool.com/courses/flatirons-classic-climb

flickr.com/James Tiffin, Jr.

Hike the Tall Trees Trail, Redwood National Park, California

LENGTH: Half-Day

DESCRIPTION: Somewhere in the Tall Trees Grove in Redwood National Park is a tree that is 379 feet tall, but you won't know which one when you're there. You probably won't much care because you'll be craning your neck and oohing and ahhing at several enormous trees when you're standing at the base of them. The identities of tall trees are kept secret to safeguard them, and in the Tall Trees Grove, you will realize the futility of trying to compare the height of 35-story-tall trees while standing at the bottom.

Unlike a lot of adventures, this hike doesn't have lots of expansive views. The appeal is experiencing the awe of standing next to Very Big Nature and enjoying the quiet of the grove of trees. The park limits access to the Tall Trees Grove to 50 visitors per day, and you'll pick up a first-come, first-served code to a locked gate at the park visitor center, 45 minutes away, before starting your hike. It's a 1.3-mile walk down to the grove and 3.7 miles total.

Rain or shine (and of course 35-story trees require lots of rain to grow that tall), the Tall Trees Trail is a one-of-a-kind day hike for all ability levels.

SEASON: Year-round

INFO: nps.gov/redw/planyourvisit/tall-trees.htm

flickr.com/russellstreet

The Dawn Patrol

© iStock.com/Doug Ash

WHILE WORKING AT THE GEAR COMPANY Black Diamond in the 1980s and 1990s, a climber and mountaineer named Alex Lowe popularized an idea called "the Dawn Patrol," which is still practiced by hundreds of people in the Salt Lake City climbing and skiing communities.

The Dawn Patrol idea was this: You work from 9 to 5. But from 5 p.m. to 9 a.m., you have 16 hours to do anything you want. So Lowe and other Black Diamond employees would get out of bed at 2 a.m. or 3 a.m. during the winter months and ski tour in the

Wasatch Mountains just a few miles from the company headquarters. They'd ski as much as they could for 5 or 6 hours and then head into work just in time. By going to bed early the night before and being willing to wake up at an hour that seems ridiculous to most people, they were able to create almost a half day of skiing right in the middle of the week.

Nowadays, plenty of people in the Salt Lake Valley do Dawn Patrols, skiing, rock climbing, and even ice climbing. And it's not just Black Diamond employees. If you have some ambition, you can do your own Dawn Patrols. You don't have to ski or climb—it's just as fun to do an early morning mission mountain biking, trail running, or hiking, and if you do the math, you'll find plenty of things you can get done before work.

Do you have time? Everyone's schedule is different, but I've seen plenty of people who have time for weekday trail runs or bike rides after work. All you're doing with the Dawn Patrol idea is shifting that same activity to before work and maybe missing a few hours of sleep. If you can swing it, you won't regret it. Early morning, no crowds, home for dinner after work, and you might find you have the feeling that you snuck one in on the universe when you're sitting in your office smugly (or not so smugly, whatever your style) at 9 a.m. with the knowledge that you spent an hour or two on your favorite trail before coming in.

You're not "making time" where there once wasn't any—you're just shifting priorities. You're trading a good night's sleep for a good morning's run, ride, or hike and seeing what it feels like. My guess is you won't regret it. Give it a shot some morning in the late spring, summer, or early fall, and see what you think. You don't have to call it a "Dawn Patrol" if you don't want to—you just have to be up early.

49

Ride the Jungfraubahn, Switzerland

LENGTH: Half-Day

DESCRIPTION: Sitting at an outdoor café table in the Swiss mountain town of Grindelwald and staring at the intimidating 6,000-foot north face of the Eiger is enough to scare anyone away from the daunting idea of ever climbing it. But from Grindelwald it is possible to climb almost 8,000 feet into a world of snowy peaks and massive glaciers without so much as breaking a sweat and to look out from inside the north face of the Eiger while you do it.

From the train station in Grindelwald, it's an 80-minute train ride on the Jungfraubahn, stopping three times at scenic overlooks (including the windows looking out the Eiger north face) to the "Top of Europe," the 11,332-foot Jungfraujoch, where you'll look down on the 14-mile-long Aletsch Glacier, the largest glacier in the Alps.

And you won't even have to carry a mountaineering axe, crampons, or a helmet: There are three restaurants, a hall of ice sculptures, shops, and an observation deck. It's not wilderness, but it's one of the most rewarding train rides you can take—anywhere.

SEASON: Year-round (but keep in mind how cold it gets at 11,000 feet in the winter)

INFO: jungfrau.ch/en-gb

flickr.com/Andrew Bowden

50

Climb the Krogerata, Telluride, Colorado

LENGTH: Half-Day

DESCRIPTION: Via ferratas are popular in European mountain ranges, but routes built on ladder rungs and steel cables attached to rock faces for the most part have not caught on in the United States, save in a handful of places. One of the most famous is Telluride's Krogerata, the via ferrata built by and named for the late Chuck Kroger, a local mountaineer.

Kroger started building the via ferrata that traverses a cliff band above town in the years before his death in 2007, and since then, it's been a bit of a local secret, mostly because of its questionable legality. But now, thanks to access easements obtained by the local Telluride Mountain Club, the 2-mile route with sheer drops beneath it is totally legal and open to everyone. It's perfect for those who want the experience of rock climbing without the gear and experience necessary and great for anyone who doesn't have a debilitating fear of heights and exposure.

The round-trip via ferrata traverse takes 4 hours from the parking lot, including the hike up to the traverse, the traverse itself, and the hike down the descent trail. Climbers will need harnesses, via ferrata leashes, and helmets, which are included with a guided trip on the Krogerata.

SEASON: May–Oct

INFO: tellurideadventures.com/summer/via-ferrata

Brendan Leonard

This Book Is Just a Start

Jason Zabriskie

THIS BOOK CONTAINS ALL SORTS OF ADVENTURES of varying lengths and has enough ideas to keep you busy adventuring around the world for more than a year if you do every single one of the trips here.

You probably won't do all the trips in this book, and believe it or not, that's a good thing. Even if you do just a few of them, my hope is that you'll gain some experience and skills and use these trips to start planning your own unique adventures. As we've covered, the popular places are popular for a reason, but there are thousands of more exciting places outside of the popular ones. See some of the best stuff, get your feet under you, and start researching your own plans.

I wrote about climbing a Colorado 14er in Full-Day Adventures chapter. That's one hike. There are 58 14,000-foot mountains in Colorado, and there are 636 13,000-foot mountains. And that's just in Colorado. We included adventures all across the United States and some in other parts of the world, but this book merely scratches the surface of what's out there. You can take a train across America (page 49), but you can also take trains across Russia, Vietnam, India, and plenty of other countries.

Don't get hung up on what you see other people doing on Instagram or what you read in magazines. Get your feet underneath you with a few of the ideas in this book, and then start to figure out your own adventures. Get some maps, read some old travel books, and start dreaming. Or just spin a globe, point your finger somewhere, and figure out something to do wherever your finger lands. Then convince a friend to join you, put down some dates, and buy some plane tickets.

No matter what you're doing, whether it's rock climbing, mountain biking, skiing, mountaineering, kayaking, hiking, backpacking, or riding trains, it's all just travel. You might be traveling halfway around the world or traveling 500 feet up a rock face somewhere (or traveling halfway around the world to travel 500 feet up a rock face). It's all folly, it's all adventure, and it can all be the time of your life. Have a great time out there.

Weekend Trip: Hike a Colorado 14er (Mount Bierstadt, 14,060 feet)

DAY 1: Travel to Denver, Colorado

- Arrive early in the day to maximize acclimation to altitude from lower-elevation cities.

- Get a hotel room in Denver (or a town farther west to sleep at higher elevation).

- Pack gear and food for hike; shop for last-minute items.

- Go to bed early to ensure predawn start next morning.

DAY 2: Summit Hike

- 4 a.m.: Wake up and eat breakfast.

- 4:45 a.m.: Leave Denver to drive to trailhead.

- 6 a.m.: Arrive at Guanella Pass trailhead, 11,670 feet.

- 6 a.m.: Begin hiking.

- 10–11 a.m.: Summit; begin hiking back down.

- Noon–1 p.m.: Arrive at trailhead; begin drive to Denver.

- 1:30–2:30 p.m.: Arrive in Denver.

DAY 3: TRAVEL HOME FROM DENVER, COLORADO

Two-Weeklong Trip: Ski the Haute Route

DAY 1: Travel to Chamonix (fly into Geneva, Switzerland, then take 3-hour train ride to Chamonix).

DAY 2: Rest day in Chamonix.

DAY 3: Acclimatization/lift skiing day in Chamonix.

DAY 4: Ski from Grands Montets to Argentière Hut.

DAY 5: Ski from Argentière Hut to Trient Hut.

DAY 6: Ski from Col des Escandies to Champex; take taxi to Verbier; ski from Verbier to summit of Rosablanche and then to Prafleuri Hut.

DAY 7: Ski from Prafleuri Hut to Dix Hut.

DAY 8: Ski from Dix Hut to Vignettes Hut.

DAY 9: Ski from Vignettes Hut to Zermatt.

DAY 10: Extra day in case of bad weather/time to ski resorts around Zermatt.

DAY 11: Travel from Zermatt to Geneva; fly home.

Weeklong Trip: Mountain Bike the White Rim Trail, Utah

DAY 1: Travel to Moab, Utah (fly into Salt Lake City, Utah + drive 4 hours to Moab, Utah OR fly into Denver, Colorado + drive 6 hours to Moab, Utah). Stay in Moab hotel.

DAY 2: Meet guides at Western Spirit Adventures in Moab; shuttle to trailhead; ride 18 miles to Airport Tower campsite.

DAY 3: Ride 27 miles to Murphy Hogback campsite.

DAY 4: Ride 21 miles to the Potato Bottom campsite.

DAY 5: Ride 14 miles to Mineral Bottom; ride shuttle van back to Moab. Hotel in Moab.

DAY 6: Travel from Moab to Salt Lake City or Denver; fly home.

Brendan Leonard has bicycled across America, traversed Wyoming's Wind River Range and Colorado's Sangre de Cristo Range on foot, bicycled across Norway's Lofoten Islands, trekked Italy's Alta Via routes, hiked the original Haute Route, spent a month and a half below the rim of the Grand Canyon, climbed big walls in Zion National Park, and skied off the summits of peaks around the West. He makes a living as a full-time freelance creative, writing articles and books, producing and directing short films, and writing on his website, Semi-Rad.com. His editorial work has appeared in *Alpinist*, *CNN*, *Outside*, *Men's Journal*, *National Geographic Adventure*, *Backpacker*, *Adventure Cyclist*, and dozens of other publications.